FV

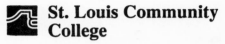

"I READ THE NEWS TODAY"

"I READ THE NEWS TODAY"

The Social Drama of John Lennon's Death

Fred Fogo

ROWMAN & LITTLEFIELD PUBLISHERS, INC.

ROWMAN & LITTLEFIELD PUBLISHERS, INC.

Published in the United States of America
by Rowman & Littlefield Publishers, Inc.
4720 Boston Way, Lanham, Maryland 20706
3 Henrietta Street
London WC2E 8LU, England

Published simultaneously in a paperback edition by Littlefield Adams
Quality Paperbacks which is available to the trade through National Book
Network. ISBN 0-8226-3034-6

British Cataloging in Publication Information Available

Library of Congress Cataloging-in-Publication Data

Fogo, Fred.
"I read the news today" : the social drama of John Lennon's death
by Fred Fogo.
p.   cm.
Includes bibliographical references (p.   ) and index.
1. Lennon, John, 1940–1980.   —Assassination. 2. Lennon, John, 1940–
—Influence. 3. United States—Social conditions —1960 –1980.
4. Baby boom generation—United States.

ML420.L38F64 1994   782.42166'092—dc20   93-48350 CIP   MN

ISBN 0-8476-7916-0 (cloth : alk. paper)

Printed in the United States of America

   TM The paper used in this publication meets the minimum requirements of
(∞)   American National Standard for Information Sciences—Permanence of
   Paper for Printed Library Materials, ANSI Z39.48–1984.

To the memory of my mother, Elizabeth Komenich Fogo, and father, Dominic Guy Fogo.

Contents

Preface

On the evening of December 8, 1980, rock star John Lennon was shot four times outside his apartment in New York City. He died in a police car en route to a hospital. His killer, Mark Chapman, surrendered at the scene without incident. Chapman said he was a fan of Lennon's and had been following him for several days. Within hours of the announcement of Lennon's death over radio and television, mourners gathered all over the world. The story dominated national and international news for days, and within a year of the killing hundreds of newspaper and magazine pieces had been written on various aspects of Lennon's life and death.

One of the persistent themes in the Lennon story was that "the sixties" had died with him: "If there were any illusions left at all for the children of the 60's, they too died Monday night," wrote Frank Rich in the *New York Times* (1980, 30). A *Newsweek* story quoted a mourner in Dallas, "It's the last nail in the coffin of the 60's" (1980, 36). Pete Hamill, in *New York* magazine, expressed it most starkly:

> At the morgue, the entrance was sealed shut with a lock and chain. Attendants with green mortuary masks moved around in dumb show, their words inaudible, or typed out forms on grim civil-service typewriters. Behind them, in a refrigerator, lay the sixties. (1980, 41)

For Lennon's fellow travelers, Christmas of 1980 offered "little cause for carolings," words Thomas Hardy used to toll the end of an earlier era. The long hair, the bright colors, the flamboyant costumes, and the street theater had been gone for some time. The young in the streets walked quickly; wool-suited and short-haired, they hunted success. There was no name for them. Later they would be tagged "Yuppies," a corruption of the sixties "Yippies." The campuses were quiet, full of grimly determined business majors already prepared to fight for increasingly scarce jobs. The music was just music, stylized and fragmented; what rebellion there was took the incomprehensible, nihilistic, and ugly form of Punk (see Marsh 1980, 1–6). The man who, as governor of California in the 1960s, threatened to give campus radicals the "blood bath" he claimed they had been asking for had been elected president of the United States in a landslide.

Of that time, one person who had come of age in the 1960s remembers:

> Around 1980 the moral center of our culture shifted from Jesus' "the last shall be first" to John Calvin's concept of the favored elect. And what we're feeling now—we who were right at the center of the culture where we fancied ourselves the radical fringe—is the unheroic, cold and nasty sensation of being truly marginal. (Gottlieb 1987, 323)

Although other themes surfaced in the writings about Lennon after his death, the prevalence and intensity of the "death of the sixties" lament provides a clue to cultural meanings in the reactions to Lennon's death by hinting at the complex relations among a historical period, a generation that shaped and was shaped by that period, and one of the most significant icons of that period and generation. Much of the writing on the death of Lennon holds the sixties, the American baby boom generation, and John Lennon and the Beatles in a delicate gravitational relationship.

Lennon's death and the commentary on it are part of a larger context of social disturbance that calls into question fundamental social meanings and relationships and sets visibly into conflict forces of stability and change. Victor Turner (1969, 1974, 1982) calls such political and cultural disturbances "social dramas." The United States in the 1960s experienced the onset of a social drama as the nation divided angrily, often violently, over the Vietnam war, the civil rights movement, and the rise of libertine lifestyles. Established values were challenged openly, and an albeit tenuous myth of national consensus was shattered along class, racial, generational, and gender lines. Even a cursory assessment of the United States in the early 1990s offers complex evidence that it still grapples with these deep divisions in a continuous ebb and flow. We fracture along so many cultural and political fault lines that traditional political party affiliations have lost their meaning, and government at the national level appears paralyzed by special-interest politics and a fickle electorate.

The writings on Lennon's death were produced largely by and for a segment of the American baby boom generation, the core of the youth rebellion of the 1960s that altered the moral and cultural landscape of American life in the 1970s and 1980s. I call this segment "the sixties generation." In the text of this book, I have chosen to spell out decades (sixties, fifties) to denote a feeling, spirit, or state of mind associated with a decade and to use numerals (1960s or 1970s) to designate specific calendrical periods. Of course, the publications I quote will not all have made the same editorial decision.

At the time of Lennon's death, members of this particular baby boom segment were ages twenty-five to forty, ranging from early to middle adulthood. They were husbands and wives, mothers and fathers; they had careers and jobs; they were almost a decade removed from the campuses and "youth ghettos" (Jones 1980) of their formative years. The various ways this segment's commentators mourned, remembered, and elegized Lennon and described and reviled his killer, Mark Chapman, reflect deep conflicts in this segment's collective and personal views of themselves, their histories, and their futures. It is an oversimplification to claim that Lennon's sudden death shocked them into adulthood, but it did spark a reflective assessment of past dreams and present realities.

In what follows, I argue that Lennon's death became an important event in the social drama of contemporary life begun in the 1960s, as an articulate if somewhat self-absorbed generational segment sought to reconcile its earlier ideals with the reality of adulthood and the particular historical and material circumstances of the 1980s and 1990s. In the context of the ruptures of the 1960s, writings on the death of John Lennon provide insights into how a segment of American society has reacted to the particular circumstances of the 1960s and 1970s. Lennon's death opened a mass-mediated space where a generational segment talked to itself about its identity and "place" in the social order through a ritual grieving process that implicitly strove for unity and consensus. However, the historical vectors that situated John Lennon and the baby boomers in the context of a fundamentally segmented society created a mixture too volatile for the creation of stable meanings.

In Chapter 1, I discuss the baby boom generation, its relationship to rock and roll and John Lennon in particular, and the generation's place in a divided society. These factors mapped out the space that shaped the elegies for John Lennon and that those elegies activated and sought to contain. In Chapter 2, I situate those strands of social conflict—particularly as they converge on Lennon's death—within the social drama perspective of Victor Turner and discuss my approach to the journalistic commentary. Turner theorizes that social drama is a process involving a serious breach of the social order. A key phase in social drama is that of redress, wherein social and cultural meanings are readjusted. The end result of social drama, Turner says, is either a reintegration of the social group under altered symbolic meaning-systems or a recognition of an irreparable social breach that results in the voluntary separation of parts of the group.

This analysis examines writings on Lennon's death in the context of the redressive phase of social drama. Chapters 3 and 4 consider writings reflecting two aspects of the separation impulse within this redressive phase: retreat to nostalgia and expression of anger or scapegoating. Nostalgic elegies to Lennon focus on him as the spirit of the youth counterculture, much in the way mourners talk about "good memories" of the deceased at a wake. Anger and scapegoating elegies attempt to "explain" the acts of Lennon's killer, Mark Chapman. They deal also with contemporary political issues such as gun control in the perceived new Reagan Era.

Chapters 5 and 6 analyze elegies suggesting modes of acceptance and reincorporation of the Lennon mourners into the larger society. One set of elegies expresses sadness and resignation and tends to refute counterculture ideals and accept the world as it is. A larger set of elegies seeks to explore how Lennon and his life could be viewed as models for incorporating counterculture ideals into the realities of aging and a changed world.

Chapters 7 and 8 cover the continuation of the counterculture's redressive phase in 1988, as Albert Goldman's debunking biography of Lennon sparked a sharp generational debate in the context of the conservative cultural wars of the 1980s.

Acknowledgments

This book is a direct outgrowth of my doctoral work in the Department of Communication at the University of Utah. I wish to thank my dissertation committee: Douglas Birkhead, Jerilyn McIntyre, Mary Strine, and Stephen Tatum.

I owe special thanks to my dissertation advisor, David Eason, who originally suggested the idea for this book and who stood by me during its creation, showing more confidence in me than I had in myself. He always knew just how far to push me. I have learned much from him about writing and teaching.

Researching this book sometimes required a Blanche DuBois approach, and I am grateful for the kindness of several strangers. Sharon Hefurth of the Dallas Public Library and Melinda McIntosh of the University of Massachusetts Library went out of their way to locate newspaper materials for me. Thanks also to Harris Worchel of the *Houston Post*, Gary Lance of the *San Jose Mercury News*, Marcia Melton of the *Fort Worth Star-Telegram*, and Sharon Bidwell of the *Louisville Courier-Journal*.

I am grateful to Westminster College of Salt Lake City, the Gore family, and my colleagues on the Professional Development Committee for providing a generous summer grant for revising the manuscript. Even though Westminster is a "teaching" school, the administration generously supports faculty research and writing projects.

My editor in Salt Lake City, Heather Bennett, has provided helpful and perceptive advice and has strengthened my writing measurably.

Most important, I thank my wife, Ronda, who has remained loving and steadfast throughout the highs and lows of this project.

Part One

The Sixties Generation, John Lennon, and Social Drama

1

John Lennon and the Sixties Generation

THE BABY BOOMERS AND THE SIXTIES GENERATION

Commentary on Lennon's death sought to make sense of John Lennon as a focal point for the intersection of various forces: the segmented nature of American society, the relationship of the baby boom generation to that society, the social upheavals of the 1960s, the cultural form of rock and roll, and the symbolic function of John Lennon. At an elemental level, these writings reflect a generational conflict. Research on baby boomers has confounded developmental sociological and psychological theories, which predicted that as the boomers aged their values would change to match those of older people. Surveys taken in the mid-1980s show, however, that boomers' attitudes still differ significantly from those of older Americans (Mills 1987, 21; see also Esler 1971 and 1984; Light 1988). Nevertheless, though the boomers are different, they are not monolithic. Almost all who mourned Lennon were boomers, but not all boomers mourned Lennon. The generation is divided among itself and in relationship to preceding and succeeding generations (Light 1988), thus adding a new dimension to the trend of segmentation in American society. A large and influential segment of boomers defined themselves in the turmoil of the 1960s while the sense of national consensus was unraveling. As meaning destabilized in the larger society, this segment created its own symbols, myths, and nostalgia. Central to that process was the cultural form of rock and roll, which established both a style and set of values pertinent to the baby boomers. From that cultural matrix John Lennon emerged as a symbolic carrier of various values and feelings associated with the sixties and with the generational segment that took its identity from that time.

The "sixties generation," therefore, is part of the larger demographic phenomenon known as the baby boom, a term that denotes both a stolid demographic fact and a more elusive concept. For a period of eighteen years from 1946 to 1964, birthrates in the United States rose in unprecedented numbers. The average of 2.1 births per woman in the 1930s soared to a peak of 3.7 births per woman by the late 1950s (Light 1988, 23). This eighteen-year period represents the single exception to a continuous two-century decline in U.S. birthrates. Fecundity increased across all social, economic, racial, religious, and geographic lines, creating a population bulge that has been compared to a pig in a python (Jones 1980, 2), an image of extreme and continual demographic distention that graphically suggests the boom generation's overwhelming force in American economics, politics, and culture.

The sheer demographic reality of the baby boom has led to several accepted generalizations about that generation. Its members grew up among many other children; although families during the boom were not large, it seemed that everyone had three children (Light, 23). The young boomers attended crowded schools and played on crowded playgrounds. Their numbers created a shortage of teachers and school rooms. They experienced great competition to get into college and, especially for later boomers, the job market. Many were raised in suburbs; indeed, G.I. Bill home loans and the development of cheap single-family homes in the suburbs are credited partially for encouraging higher birthrates (Merser 1987, 71 and 89–91). Boomers grew up in times of continued economic expansion, and a lesser percentage of their numbers knew hard times as children than had earlier generations. In the future, the nation will be hard pressed to fund their retirements and demands for medical care as they enter old age.

Other assumptions are less fastened to fact, but nonetheless compelling. The boomers have grown up with perhaps a higher degree of generational awareness than earlier demographic groups. They were among the first Americans to experience the luxuries and pitfalls of being "teenagers." Public pronouncements seemed, during the 1950s and early 1960s, to emphasize their promise, to pin great hopes on them. John F. Kennedy appealed to them in his inaugural speech, both to their sense of expectation and their sense of duty and responsibility. *Time* magazine named this "Under 25" generation its "Man of the Year" for 1965.[1] Their numbers gave them great economic power as they became teenagers and young adults. Much of television and almost all of radio catered to them, from the mid-1950s on to the present. They became prime targets for advertisers. In short, they grew up immersed in mass media that identified them and helped them, in turn, to form a sense of generational identity.

Their symbiotic relationship to the mass media allowed them to create their own languages, clothing styles, and modes of identity. Their numbers accorded them media attention, and the media attention reinforced their peer influence on each other. They were not just a television generation; they were also, among other things, a radio, record, and automobile generation. Such conditions no doubt contributed to the so-called "generation gap" in the 1960s, as huge numbers of youngsters raised in a world more economically secure and more conducive to individual choice than the world of their parents embraced increasingly different attitudes toward lifestyles and social roles (Light, 28).

Researchers have found, however, that baby boomers are hardly monolithic. They are divided by age, gender, education, economic class, and by specific historical circumstance. Though the boom generation has been more liberal on social issues than older generations, surprisingly, it has, in the past decade, displayed the greatest voting dichotomy by sex of any age group, with males favoring Republicans and females Democrats. Opinion polls show significant divisions on national issues among baby boomers classified by level of education. Less educated boomers, for example, consistently express hawkish views on foreign policy. The problem of a shrinking middle class is largely a baby boomer issue; significant numbers of them are struggling to maintain or even attain middle-class status. Another significant division among boomers is race. Proportionately more blacks served in Vietnam, and black boomers occupy the lower income and lower education strata. Black boomers, however, tend to be more politically active than white boomers and tend to identify their political self-interests more clearly (Light, 76–107).

Finally, though relatively small numbers of the entire boom generation either served in Vietnam or actively protested the war, the gulf separating these groups is huge (Light, 76). The intense differences in values and social and political orientations serve as a reminder that the deep divisions and social wounds of the Vietnam war may have had the greatest impact within the boom generation rather than between the boomers and older generations. Those who protested the war remain very liberal on almost all issues. Those who served in Vietnam are less easy to categorize. The Vietnam veterans clearly set themselves apart from all others in society in ways that combat veterans have always done, but many Vietnam vets do not fit in easily with traditional veterans' organizations such as the Veterans of Foreign Wars (VFW) and the American Legion. Vietnam vets tend to be more activist and more critical of the government, especially the Veterans Administration.

Perhaps the most significant split among boomers is the age split: the differences between early boomers, born between 1946 and 1954, and later boomers, born between 1955 and 1964. Each cohort has faced significantly different social, cultural, and economic circumstances. One crucial difference is that the young boomers did not face the Vietnam draft; another is that they suffer a fate similar to that of younger siblings in a family. While the older boomers received the larger shares of economic and social benefits, the younger boomers have had to fight for what was left. The oldest boomers finished college or high school in good economic times. Those who followed suffered more directly from the economic stagnation and inflation of the 1970s. The younger boomers are less politically active and feel less control over their lives than do early boomers (Light, 78; see also Jones 1980, 128–41).[2]

In sum, those who mourned Lennon, those I deem the "sixties generation," were, for the most part, early or "first wave" (Gottlieb 1987, 9) baby boomers. They do share much with all baby boomers. But not all baby boomers mourned Lennon or were of this sixties segment. I include in the sixties generation those born between 1940 (Lennon's year of birth) and about 1955, those who could be said to have taken much of their identities from the sixties. Though such divisions are necessarily arbitrary, this division posits that members of this particular segment lived through important formative stages of their lives during this period of turmoil.

Of course, to be one of the sixties generation involves more than pure demographics. This segment of baby boomers (and pre–baby boomers) is largely middle class and college educated. Its members willingly embraced or identified with the prevalent moods, feelings, styles, and experiences of the student New Left and/or the hippie counterculture. Their catchwords included *peace, civil rights, individual freedom,* and *nature.* Theirs was the sixties brought to life in the music of Lennon and the Beatles—a time of epiphanies:

From its earliest battle cry—"You can't trust anyone over thirty"—until the end of its brief strut on the stage of national attention, the Sixties generation saw itself as a scouting party for the new world. The "cultural revolution" it was staging would free inmates from the prison of linear thought. It was the social horticulturist whose "greening of America" would allow the post-industrial age finally to break through the crust of the Puritan past. It was the avenging angel that would destroy the evil empire of "Amerika" and free the captive peoples of the world. (Collier and Horowitz 1989, 14)

Theirs was also, to be sure, an era that strongly valorized the mere state of youth (Merser 1987; Gottlieb 1987). The generational segment includes more than those who demonstrated or who lived in hippie communities. It embraces many who were just "kids in jeans," who were borne up by the burgeoning tide of youth. Speaking for this group, Cheryl Merser remembers:

> I'd never thought of myself as a devout child of the sixties—I'd thought the real sixties kids lived in Haight-Ashbury, had stringy hair and out-of-wedlock kids named Sunshine and Etherea. It wasn't until much later that I saw just how much of the sixties message I'd absorbed without even knowing it. (1987, 103)

By the 1980s, the sixties generation could include not only those who lived brief lives as dropouts or junior revolutionaries but a great number of others who had absorbed and internalized much of the mythology of the times. Mass media build just such feelings of connection.

Yet Lennon's death and subsequent events in the 1980s and 1990s have called into question the idyllic memories of the sixties, as members of this particular segment have, or have not, come to terms with succeeding decades and their own life paths. The meaning of the sixties lies at the heart of much of the malaise and uneasiness experienced by these people. They have not yet fixed its place. Too disjointed and schizophrenic, the time does not offer solace from a troubled present. Nostalgia for the sixties "is mixed in with wistfulness, feelings of unfulfilled promise, and some bitterness" (Jones 1980, 248). The disappointment is with both the self and society. Many former, self-declared hippies lament that the Rousseauean, tribal myth of their youth has not been sustained. Some now see themselves as having led misshappen lives; they feel humbled by the contrast between their grand dreams and their present lives, both spiritually and materially. They are self-doubting and even feel foolish about their old values, which now seem discredited, or even worse, objects of derision, no longer accorded even the status of threat (Gottlieb, 325–27). Many share the feeling expressed on a T-shirt that proclaims "Stunted By The Sixties" (Gottlieb, 4). They face the problems of middle age burdened with a youth-worshiping mythic past:

> What remains from our sixties is a lingering self-consciousness in the way we express ourselves as adults that wasn't there when we were expressing ourselves as kids—a resistance to feeling like a "real" grown-up, as if real grown-ups were still the enemy. (Merser, 109)

The sixties generation, then, shares a sense of myth about itself and its defining epoch, but its members have entered adulthood and middle age less certain about the meanings of the times and the myths. Their emotions range from indulgent nostalgia to self-hate and rejection of the past. The death of John Lennon in 1980 brought much of this turmoil to the surface and helped engender a self-reflective debate.

The sixties generation and early baby boomers, however, faced more than just a spiritual crisis, as large material forces moved quietly and inexorably to destabilize them in the 1970s and 1980s. In their demographic studies of the baby boom generation, both Landon Jones (1980) and Paul Light (1988) emphasize that the surge of baby boomers entered the work force during the decade-long economic contraction in the early 1970s. The economy simply could not absorb the college-educated boomers. Jones argues that even the rapidly expanding economy of the 1950s could not have handled such a demographic assault (153). It is possible that sixties generation "dropouts" did the economy a favor, since there were few jobs for them had they decided to enter the "straight" world. The 1970s was a period of "quiet depression" (Light 1988, 51) for the boomers to the extent that it was characterized by chronic underemployment and dashed expectations. From 1969 until 1976, over 27 million college-educated boomers were forced to take jobs for which they were overtrained (Jones, 155). The problem of "growing up" for the sixties generation was not just a problem of its youth-worshiping ideology; it had to do also with difficult material conditions that postponed careers, marriages, childbearing, and home ownership for a substantial portion of an already huge demographic cohort.

Thus the sixties generation may be seen as having been caught in a double bind. Their own oppositional ideology had been called into question, and they became subject to self-doubt about it. Yet, even when and if they attempted to move back into mainstream society, their sheer numbers in combination with a contracting national economy often precluded them from taking the normal roads to social re-entry in the form of stable jobs, careers, and marriage and family. Their peculiar economic/demographic situation served to reinforce their sense of difference.

ROCK AND ROLL AND JOHN LENNON

Lennon's importance for the sixties generation, and his place in the culture, is bound up, too, with the specific history and dynamics of the popular culture form of rock and roll. Rock and roll is not a thing so much as a way of being, a gestalt that is larger than the sum of its parts. It conveys unconcious processes and feelings that work below the level of language (Blacking 1973). Its history, however brief, suggests that it both conditions and is conditioned by its total environment.

One cultural function of rock may be vestigial. Puberty rituals have provided crucial moments of transition from childhood to adulthood throughout history. Yet modern societies lack fixed puberty rituals, and the fairly recent construction of the term and concept of *adolescence* reflects a deep cultural recognition of an "in-between" period, but one that is not marked by specific ritual. Adolescence is, in modern societies, a time of intense emotion and great change, both physically and socially. If there is a culturally (not necessarily biologically) evolved need to mark this time, then the emergence of rock and roll may be explained partially as a kind of free-floating puberty rite. Rock and roll's bodily, ecstatic appeal carries in it the emotional intensity of major rituals and plunges its participants sometimes into a dark and disorderly place, what Victor Turner (1969, 1974, 1982) calls the "liminal," in-between, or threshold space of tribal rituals. Rock and roll also emerged from the liminal areas of American culture—from black rhythm and blues and gospel and from white, Southern, working-class rockabilly.

Rock and roll, of course, was coterminous with the flowering of the category "teenager" in the 1950s and of the youth culture of the 1960s. The music became the emblem and special property of the simultaneously demographic and ideological category "youth" (Frith 1978 and 1981; Grossberg 1986) and a site for antagonism among social segments. As Landon Jones observes, somewhat hyberbolically:

> The baby boomers *were* the rock audience. Rock was the sound track in the movie version of their lives. They discovered it, danced to it, romanced to it, went to college with it, protested to it, got married to it, and someday, presumably, will be buried to it. The music consolidated their group identity. . . . Rock was a language that taught the baby boom about themselves. (1980, 62)

In one of the first sixties nostalgia movies, *The Big Chill* (1983), the opening scene at a funeral service climaxes with an old college friend of the deceased pounding out an energetic and angry organ rendition of the Rolling Stones's "You Can't Always Get What You Want." As the mourners leave the chapel, the real Stones record comes over the soundtrack and punctuates the procession to the cemetery. The centrality of the music to the meaning and memories of the sixties is established immediately. The movie's appeal was enhanced by the weaving of rock music into the narrative. To examine American culture at the time of Lennon's death is to examine a culture influenced immensely by the economic, political, and cultural force of the children of rock and roll. As the older boomers and the sixties generation entered adulthood and middle age in 1980, their cohorts in the mass media elegized John Lennon in the context (among others) of twenty-five years of the shared experiences of rock and roll. And John Lennon had, by virtue of his talent and his force of personality, become one of the major figures in that brief history.

John Lennon was born in 1940 in Liverpool, England. He identified strongly with early American rock and roll. In some ways, the northern industrial areas of England shared the devalued cultural status of the American South (Curtis 1987, 133). The early English infatuation with rock and roll and the emergence of English bands came mostly from this region. Lennon liked to present himself as a kind of working-class hero, but his legacy for rock and roll and popular culture lies more in his artistic, intellectual, and verbal bent. As leader and driving creative force of the Beatles, the most successful and influential popular music group in history, Lennon became a primary force in expanding rock and roll's appeal in the mid-1960s to an increasingly large, educated, middle-class audience. (See, for example, Frith 1981, 99; 1984, 60 and 64; Goldman 1982, 356–60.) He and American folk-rocker Bob Dylan brashly insinuated rock and roll into the realm of art. Lennon's verbal wit, imaginative range, intellect, and political consciousness blurred distinctions between art and entertainment, inviting fresh critical approaches to the study of popular culture (Thomson and Gutman 1987, xiv).

Both as a Beatle in the 1960s and as a solo artist in the 1970s, Lennon became associated indelibly with the youth counterculture. By the late 1960s, the Beatles had identified themselves with hallucinogenic drug use, the anti–Vietnam war movement, and various other personal freedom and social justice causes espoused by the young New Left and the hippie counterculture. After the breakup of the Beatles in 1969, Lennon's life continued to mirror the turmoil of the times and came easily to symbolize the strange and difficult life paths of his generation. In the early 1970s, Lennon wrote political songs and engaged in numerous public demonstrations against war, racism, sexism, and political oppression. Lennon also went through the then-fashionable primal scream therapy, and in the mid-1970s his music became intensely personal, even psychotherapeutic. From 1975 until 1980, Lennon virtually dropped out of public view. He wrote little and produced no records. He and Yoko Ono had a child in 1975, thus beginning a reclusive period that Lennon liked to call his "househusband phase." In 1980, he released his first album in five years, *Double Fantasy*, a surprisingly gentle work that celebrated love and home life. It received mixed reviews. Two months later, he was shot and killed outside his New York apartment building.

Lennon stands as an appropriate cultural symbol of the sixties also because his public career mirrored the conflicted, change-oriented atmosphere of the times. He continually altered his persona and consequently risked shrinking his audience. Rock critic Jim Miller notes, "Lennon was the first superstar to keep alienating himself from the role of star" (Cocks 1980, 43). At the time of their North American conquest in 1964, Lennon and the Beatles, cast as lovable mop-tops, stood positioned to stake out the kind of expanding bubble of appeal that Greil Marcus (1975) assigns to Elvis Presley. But even at the height of their American fame in 1964, their first movie, *A Hard Day's Night*, quite openly expressed a weariness with their unprecedented mass celebrity. By 1966, Lennon made his famous, and misconstrued, remark that the Beatles were more popular than Jesus. The comment met with outrage, especially in the American South and was followed by a series of public burnings of Beatles records, instigated by local disc jockeys. *Sergeant Pepper's Lonely Hearts Club Band*, released in 1967, was taken widely to be the official anthem and manifesto of the budding hippie culture (see, for example, Brown and Gaines 1983, 218–22; Frith 1984, 60; Gitlin 1987, 216), and soon after, Lennon admitted to taking hundreds of trips on LSD. Lennon and the rest of the band openly declared their opposition to the Vietnam war.

In 1968 John left his wife and child for a Japanese performance artist, Yoko Ono. Even the most devoted Beatles fans tended to regard her as an intruder who not only destroyed Lennon's family but, even worse, broke up the band. Looking increasingly like Western representations of Jesus, Lennon appeared nude with Yoko on an album cover, and the newly married couple staged a "bed-in" for peace in Montreal. In the 1970s Lennon embarked on various activist paths and ended the decade in seclusion. He openly challenged the accepted show business goal of fame and celebrity, of seeking an ever-expanding audience and universal acceptance. He appeared, rather, to seek out controversy and conflict. His actions not only alienated parents and conservatives, those challenged by the youth culture, but also appeared to alienate and test the patience of even his most loyal fans and followers. Lennon made life difficult for his fans, for those who believed they shared with and through him a vision of the sixties. He often exhibited ambivalence about his own fame and influence, speaking against it, yet using it to draw attention to his political and social pronouncements, which often were less than perspicacious and would have drawn no attention were they uttered by an ordinary citizen (see Frith 1984, 68).

Acutely aware of his perceived importance for the sixties generation, Lennon expressed, almost a decade before his death, both disappointment and resignation about the dreams of the sixties: "The dream is over. It's just the same, only I'm thirty, and a lot of people have long hair. That's what it is man, nothing happened except that we grew up" (Wenner 1971, 41). The "dream" that Lennon declared over in 1971 is impossible to define with precision; it looked toward a changed world that would embody hazy abstractions such as *peace, love,* and *ecstasy,* but it also set a social segment apart from both its cohorts and elders. Both the "dream" and the inevitable ensuing conflict were acted out largely in the mass media.

THE SIXTIES AND A DIVIDED SOCIETY

The sixties generation and John Lennon existed, of course, in a larger culture, and for most of that culture, the "death of the sixties" may have been welcome and well overdue. For great numbers of Americans, the turmoil connoted by the term "sixties" is a source of both confusion and anger:

> Rarely in modern history has the common man had his fundamental, taken-for-granted convictions about man, woman, habits, manners, laws, society, and God—i.e. the entities of tremendous existential salience everywhere—so challenged, disrupted, and shaken. Clearly, if one can speak of a collective identity crisis, of a period of radical discontinuity in a peoples' sense of who and what they are, the late sixties and early seventies in America come about as close to realizing that condition as can be imagined. For millions it did indeed seem that the center would no longer hold. That all certainties had been rendered problematic and that a rash of moral madness had broken upon the world. (Davis 1977, 421–22)

The sixties represent a problematic site in our national identity, and legacies and reminders of the sixties have informed recent national dialogues. In the 1988 presidential race, George Bush attempted to defuse criticism of Dan Quayle's avoidance of serving in the armed forces during the Vietnam war by asserting that Quayle's national guard service was perfectly honorable and that Quayle, at least, never burned an American flag. Bush's generous criterion for qualification for the nation's second highest office seemed a designated ploy to revive old antagonisms of the sixties, both between and among generations. The nation's Vietnam trauma was addressed more directly in the 1980s with the construction of an enigmatic and controversial memorial in Washington. Several Vietnam movies in the 1980s portrayed soldiers more sympathetically than did 1970s movies. There is underway a significant sixties nostalgia wave, but most of the present reconstruction of the sixties stems from its fundamentally unresolved status and its divisiveness. One recent example bears closer analysis.

The 1987 fiasco over the nomination of Douglas Ginsburg to the Supreme Court exemplifies the conflicted legacy of the sixties and the peculiar "Sixties-within-the-Eighties" (Collier and Horowitz 1989, 15) phenomenon, as various versions of the sixties were constructed, reconstructed, and deconstructed in the 1980s. Ginsburg is possibly the first known political victim of the baby boom lifestyle (Light, 29). Selected in a hurried effort to find an ideologically pure conservative justice in the wake of the embarrassing, bitter, and divisive Senate rejection of Robert Bork, Ginsburg had several "generational skeletons" in his closet. This baby boomer conservative of the late 1980s had traveled a perfectly normal sixties generation path through the 1960s and 1970s. He was a supporter of Robert Kennedy in 1968; he had clerked for liberal Supreme Court Justice Thurgood Marshall; he had been married twice; and he—along with some 50 million other Americans—had smoked marijuana in the late 1960s and early 1970s, both as a student and a professor. In the late 1980s context of a "war on drugs," Ginsburg's past behavior, though exceedingly normal and probably tame by sixties generation standards, was seen to be scandalous, and automatically torpedoed his nomination. Though Ginsburg's present judicial views are conservative and acceptable to an older generation and to conservative baby boomers, for the older generation, his past was simply unforgivable, a reaction that reveals the lingering deep cultural divisions between the sixties generation and most of their elders. Two subsequent Supreme Court appointees, David Souter and Clarence Thomas, admitted to having smoked marijuana, and in 1992 a man who admitted to smoking marijuana but "didn't inhale" received 43 percent of the national vote and became president of the United States.

Even in the early 1990s, attitudes toward drug use point toward significant divisions, both inter- and intragenerational, but the dislocations of that earlier period may only reflect deeper strains of ideology and changing material conditions in American society. It is quite possible that the sixties did not engender divisions so much as expose and openly challenge them. The American experience has not been one of simple unity or division, as Robert Wiebe (1975) points out; rather we are a nation simultaneously held together by and separated into segments, small, compartmentalized groups with changing historical bases that cooperate with one another so as to maintain separation. In everyday practice, Americans are individualistic in terms of declaring and defining segmental values, and they are group-oriented toward their segment rather than toward the nation.

The turmoil of the 1960s brought into the open a fundamental contradiction between individual and group that has been central to the American experience. Critics of American society often divide along such lines: Progressives argue with romantics about whether we overvalue naked individualism at the expense of any coherent concept of the whole, while critical theorists focus on the problem of bland conformity and loss of individualism, enforced largely by a mind-numbing mass media. There are no clear-cut political divisions along these lines of individual versus group values; liberals and conservatives have argued from both positions.

Robert Wiebe, however, viewing America as a fundamentally segmented society from colonial times to the present, claims our cherished pronouncements of individual freedom have been generated by and for segment interests rather than in the service of a strongly developed concept of the individual. Segments fight for freedom under the rhetoric of individual rights. They tend to be strongly exclusionary and demand conformity. Segments also sometimes do engender a sense of community and communion among members.

Arguing that segments developed in the absence of entrenched privilege, in the absence of feudalism and aristocracy, Wiebe generalizes three types of segmentation characteristic of three centuries. The center of eighteenth-century society was the family in a community. The nineteenth century was a time of rapid change, and new social orders reflected that impulse. The major segmenting force of the nineteenth century was the geographic community, set in contrast to the increasing mobility and rootlessness demanded by the economic imperative to grow or die. By the twentieth century, geographical sense of place had broken down, and *what* one did came to supersede *where* one did it. With the rise of specialization and expertise, society tended to segment along work and professional lines, and new management and knowledge elites evolved.

Within this framework, Americans adopted a public language of moderation, as segments struggled for power and autonomy. The sixties ruptured this decorum; the dominant rhetorics of euphemism and conciliation were replaced by rhetorics of accusation, anger, and confrontation. The sixties called up segmentation to our national consciousness. Sharp social, racial, generational, and gender divisions seemed to tear away at an ongoing mythical consensus, but segmentation has been natural to us because it has been functional:

> As the record of the sixties demonstrates, Americans have cultivated their differences, hatreds, and barriers. As a much longer record demonstrates, Americans have also built a remarkably resilient society capable of surviving crises with considerably greater impact than the one in the sixties. (Wiebe 1975, 13)

I should add emphasis to Wiebe's assertion that we have had greater crises than the sixties. Certainly the Civil War ranks as our greatest, longest-lasting social drama. Also, the 1890s and the 1930s probably equal or exceed the sixties in social and political turbulence.

Many critics and defenders of mass media would claim that media may be the reason for the resiliency noted by Wiebe. Carlin Romano describes the role of the press in the tenuous balance of order and disorder thusly:

> It may be that our mixed society maintains relative internal peace only because so many differences are masked behind a journalism that discourages the vocabulary of class, race, and ideology. If every newspaper here took an openly partisan position, closer to the model of Italian and French journalism, we might face a far more conflict-ridden society. (1986, 75)

Each day mass media struggle to maintain a coherent cultural map. News, according to Herbert Gans (1979), has to do largely with perceived threats to the social consensus. The commonplace "domestic disorder" news story is characterized by its emphasis on efforts of public officials and institutions to restore order and thus becomes very quickly a story of "order restoration" (54–55). Yet this very tendency of news toward "restoration of order" reveals that the daily newspaper or newscast is a site where groups in society struggle over the definition of what is real.

The sixties were a time of division and dislocation, but not because America fell prey to alien social and ideological microbes. Various changes such as new communication and production technologies; the presence of a huge, educated youth population; and the government's decison to pursue an unpopular war provided fissures through which old and taken-for-granted divisions welled to the surface of our social consciousness. Mass media gave voice to an increasingly influential "adversary culture" (Schudson 1978, 179) in the sixties and brought these divisions to the national attention. Relationships among the news media, the government, and the media's audience ruptured during the 1960s and 1970s (Eason 1988, 221), thus contributing to the sense of disorder; but simultaneously, the mass media strove, by virtue of their structures and practices, to contain and make sense of events in the service of consensus. They provided horizontal paths of communication among segment members and vertical paths of communication in the service of consensus.

The dramas of our society play themselves out daily in our newspapers and on our televisions and radios, where the various conflicts take on form and voice. For we know our worlds through communication. We produce our worlds in symbols and then settle in to live in them. We work much to maintain what we produce. Our reality constantly breaks down: "People get lost physically and spiritually, experiments fail, evidence counter to the representation is produced, mental derangement sets in—threats all to our models of and for reality that lead to intense repair work" (Carey 1975, 17).

Mass communication acts simultaneously in vertical and horizontal vectors in the production of reality. Mass media carry vertical or centripetal forces of unity and consensus and also horizontal or centrifugal forces of segmentation and difference (Carey 1969). The mass media affirm our sense of collective identity and also cater to our individual and group-identity selves. We are called together in one spirit, of one mind, to mourn the assassination of a president, and we flip the channel selector or browse the magazine stand to link ourselves with discrete groups with whom we share interests and experiences. As Carey argues, above all, mass communication should be viewed as a dramatic form in which "a particular view of the world is portrayed and confirmed" (1975, 8).

To read a newspaper, for example, is to enter a field of dramatic action and to participate in a world of contending forces. The newspaper is a cultural text like a play, a novel, or even a Balinese cockfight that gives daily life some form and order. The 1960s were a time of great strain for the sense-making mechanisms of our culture. Our worlds, our maps of reality, seemed constantly threatened in the sixties, but perhaps they always are in such danger.

The conflicts and segmentation of contemporary society are evident every day in our mass media, and this study focuses on one area of the conflicted legacy of the sixties. The social drama perspective of Victor Turner provides ways of assigning meaning and form to the particular generational conflict I find in writings on the memory of John Lennon. A segment's self-doubt and its conflicts with other segments are seen in the larger context of the breakdown of and struggle over meaning. Writings on Lennon reflect not only generational concerns but also a complex relation among society, media, and culture. The social drama perspective provides a means for analyzing a particular cultural discourse in a broad societal context.

NOTES

1. In the late 1980s, the sixties and baby boomers were subjects of cover stories in *Time* (May 19, 1986; January 11, 1988; September 4, 1989), *Newsweek* (October 17, 1988; July 3, 1989), *People* (August 15, 1988; August 22, 1988), and *Life* (August 1989).

2. Lennon's killer, Mark Chapman, and President Ronald Reagan's would-be assassin, John Hinckley, are both of this late boomer cohort. See Jones (1981).

2

Social Drama Theory and the 1960s

Social reality can be said to exist in ongoing dramas that affirm and adjust shared symbols. The mass-mediated mourning for John Lennon is part of an ongoing drama of the creation and maintenence of social order, and it suggests the presence of the ongoing phenomenon of social drama. The sixties generation took much of its identity from those times of conflict and confrontation when its members challenged authority and the meaning system that legitimized that authority. A decade after its time of origin, members of this segment found themselves in changed circumstances, unsure of their previous ideals and of their place in the social order they originally had rejected. Elegies for John Lennon reveal a social segment grappling with problems of its own identity and its relation to the larger social order.

SOCIAL DRAMA THEORY

Victor Turner argues that to detect and analyze social drama is in great part to study communicative acts. Turner says social drama is observed retrospectively by looking at communication and studying symbols (1974, 37). Social drama may be inferred, then, from various cultural texts, and, in modern times, such inference requires exploring the various relationships between mass media and culture.

We create our social reality by putting symbols together to make stories or dramas. Turner developed the concept of "social drama" to describe a transcultural phenomenon by which cultures reveal their fundamental tensions, their meaning systems, and their relations of power. The social drama is "a spontaneous unit of social process and a fact of everyone's experience in every human society" (1982, 68),

19

and "It can be isolated for study in societies at all levels of scale and complexity" (1974, 33). Social dramas occur within groups that share values and some sense of common history. They may occur at the level of group, village, or nation: A Ndembu marriage dispute and Watergate are social dramas. As a process, social drama can be seen in retrospect to have structure. It reveals a temporal structure of phases that reveal goals (1974, 37).

The temporal phases of social drama consist of (a) a *breach* of a norm that is so serious as to engender a (b) *crisis* where conflict occurs and common meanings are called into question. This conflict often reveals deeper levels of social structure and the sets of oppositions and tensions that support them. Crisis requires various processes of (c) *redress*, which may involve political and legal efforts or performance of public ritual. Rituals of redress often involve scapegoating. Turner emphasizes that redress requires the creating, reformulating, and testing of cultural meaning. It is here in overt public expression that Turner believes social change may be studied by analyzing the redressive machinery brought to bear on a crisis. This phase reveals the fullest expression of both pragmatic and symbolic efforts. Here, society is most self-conscious (1974, 41). The last phase of social drama reveals one of two possible conclusions: (d) *reintegration* of conflicting groups, with altered relations and meanings, or *social recognition of irreparable breach*, which usually leads to voluntary separation of elements of the group (1982, 70–71).

In Turner's view, social drama may subsume ritual. In viewing ritual in the context of "social drama" Turner focuses on ritual as part of the range of potential responses to breach and crisis, as a dynamic form always "shedding and gathering meaning over time and altering in form" (1982, 27). Turner's concepts of the *liminal* and *liminoid* provide theoretical avenues for exploring ritual aspects of mass media and mass cultural forms in the redressive phase of the social drama of contemporary life.

LIMINALITY

Studying an isolated African tribal culture, Turner found great tension and complexity in rites of passage ceremonies. In these rituals Turner found (furthering the work of Arnold van Gennep, [1908] 1960) what he called a "liminal phase." The term liminal is derived from the word *limen*, which means "threshold." Thus it suggests a symbolic passageway. The individual in this phase experiences a suspended identity and sense of reality. This in-between place, culturally sanctioned via the ritual form and culturally necessary for the success of the ritual, is a breeding ground for change.

In modern heterogeneous societies the in-between areas are found in various forms of leisure and entertainment, rather than in the less visible and less influential forms of social ritual. Modern in-between forms include theater, poetry, novel, ballet, film, sport, rock music, classical music, art, and pop art, among others. These "liminoid forms," as Turner calls them, "play with the factors of culture" (1982, 40) and are not contained, as are liminal rites in tribal cultures, precisely because the established order is less oppressive in modern societies where people have much more choice in almost every aspect of daily life. The ritual aspects of redress in contemporary social dramas, Turner argues, will be enacted to a great extent in these liminoid, mass-mediated areas, as is the case in the death of John Lennon.

STRUCTURE/ANTISTRUCTURE

Social drama is driven by a fundamental, dialectical tension between two states or modes of being: structure and antistructure. The social drama surrounding Lennon's death has much to do with Lennon's and the sixties generation's perceived relationships with both states, with what appears to be an as-yet-unresolved dialectical tension in the sixties generation between these two modes of being.

Structure refers to the patterned arrangements of role, status, and status sequences—status sequences referring to what is studied, for example, in life cycle or developmental psychology, the dividing lines between childhood, adolescence, adulthood, and old age (Turner 1974, 237). In an existence defined by structure, individuals take their identities from their social roles and subordinate their impulses to prevailing norms. Structure, in short, is what makes things work among people. Structure keeps us driving on the right side of the road and makes us send our children to school. In structure, we both unconsciously and willingly restrain some of our impulses for a perceived greater good for the whole and partly because of fear of social sanctions. Structure is essential for any social order, from the tribe to the postindustrial nation state.

Antistructure occurs in liminal (tribal ritual) or liminoid (modern art and entertainment) experiences that upset and invert order and structure. The special feelings or emotions associated with these experiences are *communitas*. Through communitas, then, antistructure experiences provide an intensity of shared emotion not generally found in the various forms and practices of structure, which remains, for the most part, rational or taken for granted. Liminoid forms of popular entertainment and culture (both high and low) have great potential for changing the means and content of human relationships, primarily because these forms are separated from direct industrial production and from what little remains in modern societies of ingrained ritual. Liminoid forms are voluntary, which endows them with the pleasure that, in turn, augments their intensity and absorption into consciousness (1974, 16). In modern societies, communitas tends to form in the liminoid.

COMMUNITAS

Turner uses the term communitas to refer generally to the *emotional* component of the antistructure experience. The emotions of communitas take form around available cultural forms and symbols. Communitas is of the culture it confronts, and its emotional intensity inhibits its staying power. Communitas historically "declines and falls" into structure and law (1969, 132). As groups based in communitas by necessity change, what may seem to be hypocrisy is simply "a reasoned response to an alteration in the scale and complexity of social relations" (1969, 147; see also 1974, 50).

The experience of communitas is deep, sometimes mystical, but it must be temporary if society is to maintain its functions and order (1974, 274). Turner offers the history of the Franciscan order of the Roman Catholic Church as a case study of the cycle of communitas. Born in an intense emotional cauldron of spontaneous communitas and wedded to an ideal of poverty directly set against certain ideological and practical foundations of structure, the Franciscan order has necessarily shifted over time to a base in structure, as the originating emotions have subsided during a long history of changing social conditions (1969, 140–65).

Communitas also has its dark and magical sides, according to Turner. Since order is turned upside down or is even nonexistent in liminality, symbols and metaphors in that state become "dangerously ambiguous" (1974, 273). Sin and evil often accompany communitas. Highly ritualized societies provide for this danger through elaborate ritual structure. In the modern liminoid, however, the dark side of communitas may develop unchecked, as evidenced by the bloody deeds of the Manson Family in 1969—a group that exhibited classic signs of communitas.

Communitas also brings out the shaman, or, equally, the shaman functions in liminal space. In the modern world, Turner assigns shamanistic functions to poets, writers, and religious prophets, among others. At times, he argues, they are "exceptionally liminal thinkers" and he hypothesizes that just before "outstanding limina" of history (e.g., major crises of societal change) these thinkers would express major conceptual or foundation metaphors for the changed society (1974, 28). In tribal cultures, shamans exist in liminal regions; neither doctors nor priests, they are special kinds of spiritual healers with both benign and malevolent powers (Eliade 1964). Even in highly structured tribal societies they sometimes do not "fit" precisely into the order (Taylor 1985, 36–37). Shamans are healers, but they often heal via disturbances. They take their healing power from the liminal in order to set things aright in the structural, or perhaps to set change in motion that will heal the sickness in the structure. As "fine tuner of the psyche of his tribe" (Taylor, 18), the shaman's function is essentially reintegrative among the underworld, the upperworld, and the shaman's special private world that allows him the gift of access to the other worlds. The shaman deals often in the ecstatic, and in her very being can be assumed to be closely allied with communitas, the liminal, and antistructure. The shamanistic possiblities of Beatlemania were suggested by a perplexed John Lennon, who remarked about their first world tours, "It seemed we were just surrounded by cripples and blind people all the time. And when we would go through the corridors, they would be touching us" (Lahr 1981, 22–23).

Turner's theory provides a basis for a study of cultural meaning in the death of John Lennon: the concepts of antistructure, liminality, and communitas offer a context for understanding the sixties, the sixties generation, John Lennon, and the acts of remembering and elegizing Lennon. Turner himself made some of these connections in *The Ritual Process* (1969).

COUNTERCULTURE COMMUNITAS

In *The Ritual Process*, published during the height of the hippie culture, Victor Turner made several specific references to the hippie movement as an antistructure impulse. Turner observed that "the hippies' emphasis on spontanaiety, immediacy, and 'existence' throws into relief one of the senses in which communitas contrasts with structure. Communitas is part of the now; structure is rooted in the past and extends into the future through language, law, and custom" (1969, 112–

13). Indeed the hippies saw themselves, and were seen by others, as annihilators of history (Collier and Horowitz 1989; Mailer 1968; Turner 1974, 262–63).

As with earlier liminal groups such as holy mendicants and millennials, the hippies, Turner emphasized, chose certain status reversals. They retreated into the interstices of the social structure by occupying its lowest rungs and living at the margins—socially, economically, and geographically (Turner 1969, 125). As the Beats before them, they sought to re-create lost ritual traditions for the appearance of spontaneous communitas, transformative experience based in shared ecstacy. For the hippies, argues Turner, ecstacy was seen as *the* end of human endeavor (1969, 139). Herein lay the weakness at the heart of the counterculture, which Turner, among many others, was quick to see. Not only was there no structure in hippie communitas; there was, in its heyday, no ideology. As early as 1970, a member of that culture wrote:

> It is impossible to describe our "ideology," for we simply didn't have one. . . . I guess we all agreed on some basic issues—the war is wrong, the draft is an abomination and slavery, abortions are sometimes necessary and should be legal, universities are an impossible bore, LSD is good and Good For You, etc., etc.—and I realize that marijuana, that precious weed, was our universal common denominator. And it was the introduction of formal ideology into the group which eventually destroyed it, or more properly split it into bitterly warring camps. (Mungo [1970] 1982, 473)

The fundamental problem with the counterculture, according to Turner, "was a tendency among many people, especially those under thirty, to create a communitas and a style of life contained within liminality. . . . Instead of the liminal being a passage, it seemed to be coming to be regarded as a state" (1974, 261).

A similar theme is picked up by Todd Gitlin (1980), who argues that the liminoid was not the place to launch political change. The liminoid atmosphere produced "an apocalyptic, polarized political mood" (202) that, along with its "weird symboisis" (235) with the mass media, served to undermine specific political agendas of the New Left. The euphoria of dramatic, symbolic action could not be sustained according to Gitlin (159). In assessing the political failures of the sixties generation, Paul Wachtel (1989, 185) concludes: "What distinguishes a movement from a fad is the creating of sustaining structures that keep people bound together in commitments." In a very real sense, to have lived as a member of the sixties generation and to have remembered those times in 1980 was, as Turner and others suggest, to confront the troubling prospect of having planned a Life in the Liminoid. Having formed personal and collective identities in antistructure, in the grandiose dreams of universal peace, love, and harmony that existed only in communitas, many members of the sixties generation grappled with what it meant to adapt to structure. Their struggle, reflected in writings on Lennon's death, centered on perhaps the deepest conflict we can have: the question of who we are and what our lives mean. Expressions of this conflict depended upon mediated images and experiences, on memory and the construction and reconstruction of images and feelings. Much of the generational discourse focused on mediated messages in the songs and television and movie images of Lennon and the sixties.

THE SOCIAL DRAMA OF CONTEMPORARY LIFE

This study is not "about" the sixties; rather, it argues that we live now in a social drama that became evident in the 1960s. I have, to this point, offered evidence that suggests implicitly a situation of social drama—a portrait of a large, unique, and somewhat disaffected generation and a divided society that struggles to this day with various cultural and political legacies of the 1960s. Contemporary life in the United States reveals ongoing tensions that can be traced to trends and events of the 1960s. Victor Turner postulated that such a state of affairs could well be evidence of social drama. It would indicate that the ordinary legal and judicial means of conflict resolution had broken down and that at the heart of that ongoing tension and conflict would lie a crisis of meaning. Social drama describes a particular kind of "deep" conflict in which the society's very meaning system is called into question. Social drama occurs when the meaning system of a social order is shaken and conflicts are of such magnitude and depth that they challenge the ultimately fragile sets of assumptions that hold the social order together, what Clifford Geertz calls "webs of significance" (1973, 5).

The social order is challenged when great numbers of people (usually arrayed variously in groups or segments and often identifying with more than one) no longer share a concept of a social whole, when the category of "we" is unclear or contested. Under such conditions individual identity becomes problematic also, for Turner's assumption of the social construction of reality supposes that one cannot really know "me" without some concept of "we."

At the heart of the social drama of contemporary life lies the fundamental crisis that society has become "unknowable" (see Carey 1989, 266). In discussing the problems of writing journalism history in the present (ca. 1985), James Carey argues (1985, 39) that the convergence of various large social forces by the 1960s brought about "changes in the categories through which people identify themselves and work their experience into knowledge." This period of "social disorganization" is characterized by "a loosening of the coordinates of individual identity" (1985, 39), and such disorganization sets off various social movements by which people construct new definitions of both themselves and their worlds. Carey says that the social disorganization of the 1960s was not unique. The 1890s were another such period for Americans. In that time the forces of industrialization, urbanization, and democratization changed the old bases of identity in religion, region, community, and agricultural work. These categories "no longer served to describe people's experience to themselves, including their experience of themselves" (1985, 39). The various social movements of the 1890s, such as populism, progressivism, nativism, and temperance, reflected new ways of fitting into the world, new ways of answering the question "who am I?"

Carey says that a new set of social forces in post–World War II America resulted in the shift from a blue-collar to a pink- and white-collar work force, large-scale movements to the suburbs, and new patterns of social and geographic mobility. In these new contexts the older modes of identification such as ethnicity and religion altered, and some identifications such as loyalties to cities, regions, political parties, institutions, and occupations clearly waned in the 1960s (1985, 39). As intellectual and social identity became reorganized in the 1960s, new social movements emerged. Carey mentions race and gender as two significant new forms of identity to emerge in the 1960s; others have suggested the rise in the 1960s of a new professional/managerial class that complicated older individual and collective identity coordinates (Bazelon 1967; Ehrenreich 1989; Gouldner 1979). Of course, the identity form of "youth" is indelibly associated with the sixties.

Carey makes the point that all who have lived through this period and have had to refigure personal identities in relation to these social movements end up seeing history, and being situated in history, differently. The relationship between John Lennon and the sixties generation is certainly one particular, situated place from which to view the social disorganization of the 1960s. The generational memory that coalesced around John Lennon is primarily white and middle class, and gender is only a peripheral concern, emerging in some writings in the wake of Lennon's death that address the generation's particular patterns of sexism. The generation can easily be seen as self-absorbed and self-indulgent in that the perceived problems of the sixties generation seem minor compared with other groups in America, not to mention the miserable millions of the Third World. Yet, the sixties generation ought not to be dismissed as a subject of cultural inquiry. The generation was essential to social redefinitions of identity concepts such as *student, child, middle class, liberal,* and *educated.* It suggested new categories such as "student activist" and "hippie," and, at its zenith, proposed that "youth" be given the status of a social class (Gitlin 1987; McConnell 1987). Whether or not the sixties generation has always been a commendable or sympathetic character, it plays a leading role in the contemporary social drama.

Carey suggests, very much in keeping with the paradigm of social drama, that we still are working out the new social distinctions of the 1960s and that it is too early (1985) to tell which will prevail as primary identity markers. But we will, according to Carey, "produce a new symbolic social structure" (40) out of the social disorganizations that erupted in the 1960s. The desired result, says Carey, is an "enlarging of the human community with which we identify" (41). Carey describes here what Turner calls the redressive phase of social drama and its ultimate end-goal of reintegration in the social order. In the redressive phase, political, legal, and cultural "machinery" are brought to bear on the crisis.

The specific crises involve open conflicts, but the redressive period involves the creating, reformulating, and testing of cultural meaning, which, even in subsequent reintegration, can never be the same. The deeper crisis is one of shared meaning, so the goal of redress is, as Carey suggests, to create a new symbolic order. The social dislocations of the sixties are what Carey and Turner see as one of the periodic adjustments to the symbolic social structure, to the very ways of defining and comprehending the self and the world.

The social disorganization of the sixties did not commence in a single breach. The year 1968, however, is a useful marker for a series of breaches that opened up into a sense of national crisis. That year saw the Tet offensive in Vietnam, the political demise of President Lyndon Johnson, the assassinations of Martin Luther King and Robert Kennedy, riots and conflagrations in urban ghettos, student demonstrators taking over university buildings and burning the American flag, the continuing growth of a youth counterculture that openly rejected conventional values, violence and disorder at the Democratic National Convention in Chicago, victorious American athletes at the Olympics giving a Black Power salute in rebuke to the national anthem, and the bitter and divisive battle for the presidency among Richard Nixon, Hubert Humphrey, and George Wallace.

The events of that year reveal the social order rupturing into crisis—that phase of social drama that is characterized by side-taking, enmity, and reciprocal violence (Turner 1985, 125). Crisis, says Turner, often reveals "turning points or moments of danger and suspense when a true state of affairs is revealed, when illusions are dispelled and masks torn off or made impossible to don" (215). Turner describes here the shattering of a myth of consensus, the demise of a public discourse that masks divisions and enmity that marked the late 1960s. This atmosphere of contention reveals struggle over fundamental symbols and meanings, such as the nation's flag, that formerly served to unite. There is no clear line between crisis and redress (1985, 187–97), according to Turner. As various mechanisms for repairing the social structure are set in motion in redress, the enmity that characterizes crisis is still present. At some point, though, the impulse toward reintegrating the social order begins to emerge in the public dialogue.

In his acceptance speech following the 1968 election, Richard Nixon recalled a campaign stop somewhere in Ohio that year: a young girl held up a hand-written sign that said "Bring Us Together." Nixon said he hoped his presidency would help to bring America together again. Questions of sincerity aside, that Nixon or his aides would point to this example indicates that they read something in the national psyche; an impulse, at the height of crisis, toward redress. In his campaign, Nixon had tried to show himself as the middle road between the right-wing populist extremism of George Wallace and the mass media associations of student leftists and Black Power advocates with the Democratic Party that emerged from the Democratic convention. Nixon claimed to speak for a "silent majority" of "middle Americans" (we may surmise new identity forms suggested in these terms) who sought a return to normalcy. Nixon, of course, became the focal point of divisiveness as he resigned in disgrace after the Watergate affair, but there can be little doubt that he and many who voted for him in 1968 saw his presidency implicitly as a step toward redress. This redressive impulse seems constant in succeeding presidents, all of whom have in their own terms professed a desire to bring Americans back together.

Though we have had two decades of relative civil peace in contrast to the riots, demonstrations, and street politics of the 1960s, the social order still is fractured into vocal segments that have, in some ways, turned the street politics of the sixties leftists and black activists into a more sophisticated single-issue politics practiced by both liberal and conservative segments based variously on age, race, gender, geography, religion, occupation, and class. Single-issue politics became the province of political action committees (PACs), highly organized lobbyists, and the mass media. Although segments have returned to "the system" to obtain their ends, they tend to focus their efforts narrowly so that fewer and fewer voices appear to speak for that elusive concept we call "the public good." This state of affairs suggests a state of redress in which crisis has subsided but where there is yet no clear path toward consensus and reintegration.

Members of the sixties generation have been important players in the contemporary social drama. It is they who initiated many of the cultural challenges that marked the era of social dislocation, and their group consciousness was born in this period of collision of generations when they created their own world, a youth culture born in the liminoid spirit of communitas. John Lennon's death and his symbolic function after his death became important for this particular group because Lennon represented something fundamental to their sense of identity and their relations to the social order. We may better understand the social drama of the present by looking closely at how members of one segment in that drama have attempted to make sense of their own experiences and how they have struggled with their personal and collective identities in an "unknowable" society.

METHOD AND ORGANIZATION

CULTURAL TEXTS

In this study, I focus on written commentary that followed Lennon's death.[1] I gathered newspaper and magazine pieces written on John Lennon and his murder between 1980 and 1988. Most items were referenced in the *New York Times, Washington Post,* and *Los Angeles Times* indexes and in the *Reader's Guide to Periodical Literature,* and *Social Science Index.* I also obtained pieces on Lennon's death by writing to over forty daily newspapers in various parts of the country and requesting materials from their libraries. I collected approximately 200 pieces and use 116 in my analysis. There are two reasons for the disparity between the number of pieces collected and the number used. First, I tried in my initial research to focus only on "elegaic" articles and commentary, but I could not always guess content from titles. Also, some newspapers and libraries sent me everything they had about Lennon's death. The vast majority in such instances were pieces that did not fit into my analysis categories because they were either hard news or artistic evaluations of Lennon's work. A few were so general as to be virtually meaningless to me for purposes of analysis. There is, of course, some double or triple referencing. I do not propose that entire pieces fit into a single category, although some do. Longer pieces such as Ken Kesey's in *Rolling Stone* and Pete Hamill's in *New York* magazine reflect elements of two or three categories of my analysis.

The number of primary source pieces used per analytical categories is as follows: Withdrawing to the Past (Chapter 3), 16; Scapegoating and Anger (Chapter 4), 41; Resignation (Chapter 5), 7; Acceptance and Reintegration (Chapter 6), 21; The 1988 Battle over the Memory of John Lennon (Chapter 7), 27; The Sixties Generation in the 1980s (Chapter 8), 17.

My analytical focus is on commentary, feature articles, editorials, and letters to editors, not on "straight news" reports. This study, then, is not of what is thought of conventionally as journalistic practice. It emphasizes, rather, a certain portion of what James Carey (1987) calls the "corpus of journalism," the portion where journalism edges over into the realm of cultural commentary. In this context, Carey argues, journalism becomes more of a "curriculum" (151):

> The corpus includes not only the multiple treatments of an event within the newspapers—breaking stories, follow-ups, news analysis, interpretation and background, critical commentary, editorials—but also other forms of journalism that surround, correct, and complete the daily newspapers: television coverage, documentary and docudrama, the news weeklies and journals of opinion and finally, book-length journalism. (1987, 151)

The discourse on Lennon's death is a prime example of the development of a corpus of journalism, an example of Carey's assertion that journalists "devote much of their energy to . . . keeping significant events afloat long enough so that interpretation, explanation, and thick description can be added as part of ongoing development" (1981, 151). The Lennon story was "kept afloat" for about three months in the daily newspapers and for almost a year in magazines.

The journalistic texts I chose to study are part of this corpus, but they also exist in other contexts that need to be addressed. Pertinent questions about the texts chosen for analysis include: (a) What kinds of texts are cited and analyzed? (b) Where do these texts appear? (c) Who wrote them, and what status, authority, and relationship to the audience may be inferred? These texts are deeply contexted, and certainly they are not "innocent." To interpret is to make choices, to give life to some voices and to silence others. I will explain my choices and allow also, I hope, for the reader to see where I do not go and what I do not or cannot explain.

What kinds of texts are cited and analyzed? The various texts cited and analyzed range widely from twenty-five-word letters to the editor to full-blown essays by literary figures. In between are columns, features, and editorials. They do not, then, represent a particular form in the strict sense of the term (e.g., the form of the sonnet or haiku, or the form of the editorial or news report).

Where do these texts appear? These texts appear in a wide range of publications from the *New York Times* to the *Cincinnati Enquirer*, from *New York* magazine to *Rolling Stone* to *People*. I did seek a regional and status balance in gathering material. I did not want to use only texts from major national newspapers and magazines. As it turns out, the Lennon story did "play Peoria" fairly well. The publications listed above address widely differing audiences, so it may be inferred that the Lennon story had a wide appeal across the various complex geographic, economic, ideological, and demographic categories that constitute newpaper and magazine readership. This situation suggests that (a) the story was dramatic and traumatic enough and involved a celebrity significant enough to have at least short-term appeal across society (as is evidenced in the deep, though brief in comparison to written media, television coverage) and (b) the sixties generation, for whom the death prompted a grieving process, was itself scattered about in various economic, demographic, and ideological positions to some extent.[2]

Who wrote these texts, and what status, authority, and relationship to the audience may be inferred? To some extent there was a simple, self-selecting process at work as to who wrote about Lennon. As it broke, the story was assigned to the crime beat, but almost immediately it became a music, entertainment, and culture and society beat story. Many, of course, had something to say. In dailies across the country, regular columnists, reporters, and feature writers offered their thoughts, feelings, and memories. Nationally syndicated columnists joined the chorus, too.

The longer and more reflective newspaper and magazine pieces, however, were produced mostly by a special class of writers who covered rock and roll. They were, for the most part, Lennon's demographic cohorts, and a good many of them had met Lennon. They were "insiders" to Lennon and to the heady world of rock and roll. Occupying positions of status and authority, they regularly mediated records, performances, and personalities for their audiences. They were arbiters and interpreters for their special audiences in *Time, Newsweek, Rolling Stone,* the *Village Voice,* and *New York* magazines.

These writers, though, have a different relationship with their audiences than do writers, reporters, and broadcasters who cover what we tend to call serious news—politics, wars, disasters. Journalists covering political figures, for example, may admire them and like them. If a politician dies, they may write of him or her with great emotion, even love. But they are not *fans* of politicians. The word fan is rooted in the word *fanatic.* Political journalists violate the standards of their own concepts of "objectivity" if they become fans of a political figure. Gay Talese (1966) notes that the *New York Times,* "awed by what was official," covered the U.S. Senate "with drab restraint" (295) and discouraged injections of style or portrayal of human mannerisms in national political coverage. "This was not true," says Talese, " of *Times* reporting on the *un*official phases of American life. . . . It seemed so much easier for a *Times* man to write honestly and frankly about Arthur Miller than about Senator Wayne Morse" (296). Rock and roll and popular culture writers, on the other hand, have such license precisely because the stakes for them are not perceived to be so high. Conventional wisdom tells us that worshiping Hitler or Mussolini (whose relations with the masses resembled relations between fans and stars) can have disastrous results. Worshiping John Lennon or Bob Dylan in the sense that fans do appears to present little threat to the social order.

What these rock and roll and popular culture writers share with their readers, then, is a kind of fandom, a set of common experiences. Rock-and-roll critics and their readers hear the same music in their homes and on the radio and share the simultaneously personal and communal experiences of rock and roll in very similar ways. These writers share more with their readers generally than do national political writers embedded in the special world "inside the Beltway." They are fans and reflect that status, but in their power to speak as "primary definers" (Hall et al. 1978, 58) they also refract experience by establishing initial definitions or primary interpretations of topics. Other fans may put forth their own interpretations, but they have to struggle with and within the power of these initial interpretations.

In choosing to focus on ritual functions of the corpus of journalism, I examine (with the exception of a number of pieces on Lennon's killer, Mark Chapman) texts that reflect a broadly elegaic tendency. In situating these texts in the redressive arena of a social drama, I lean, naturally, toward those that consciously seek to attribute cultural meaning to Lennon and to the act of his assassination. I use the term "elegy" to describe this discursive tendency because it connotes a more broadly cultural endeavor than the term "eulogy," which is more individual and funereal. Elegy is more poetic and more culturally contexted than eulogy. The elegaic voice speaks for a group and seeks to affirm group values.

Yet these elegies are also part of a redressive phase characterized by conflict over the creation of meaning. In this context, they are best viewed as a series of claims and counterclaims that reflect generational sentiment and refract their cultural context by also providing models for grieving and making meaning. Turner emphasizes the tentative mood of redress. It is when groups struggle that heretofore submerged power relations and alliances may become unmasked. But redress also holds out promise in its liminal aspects, which may result in an extreme clarity that points to new models for the future (1974, 39–41). The discourse on the death of John Lennon qualifies, I believe, as a kind of mass culture form that embodies extreme tensions between power and possibility. We may postulate the emergence of cultural meaning in the dynamic tensions between segmentation and consensus that characterize both mass media and mass culture practices and productions.

VOICES OF SEPARATION AND REINTEGRATION

I base my analysis of the writings on Lennon on Turner's key assertion that social drama is a process, that social dramas do move toward resolution. Those resolutions are either a reintegration that always involves altered relations or an agreement to separate. I have organized the writings on Lennon within the context of the social drama of contemporary life, since I believe the social drama paradigm has value to the extent it can account for the largest field of phenomena and that my own analysis is valuable to the extent it can relate the texts in question to the social whole rather than just to a single segment. Elegaic writings on Lennon and the notion of the death of the sixties had to do with what Lennon meant to the sixties segment, with the sixties segment's collective sense of themselves and the meaning of their shared experiences and symbols, and with the relation of this segment to the larger society. In calling the segment into being once more on the occasion of Lennon's death, various spokespersons for the sixties generation proposed various meanings. Turner theorizes that the redressive phase does eventually move to resolution, and I argue that elegies for Lennon suggest paths toward both possible ends of redress—separation and reintegration.

In Chapters 3 and 4, I examine how some writers called the sixties generation together in the name of Lennon to redraw boundaries between it and the larger society. These kinds of arguments can be seen as continuations of the crisis phase, where boundaries between groups are clearly drawn. If redress is to end in separation, then it might be expected that some, or even much, discourse in the redressive phase would mark a refinement and continuation of boundaries drawn in the crisis phase. Elegies for John Lennon express separation in two modes: nostalgia and anger.

Voices of collective nostalgia reflect a fundamental tenet of the counterculture proposed by LSD guru Timothy Leary—that of passively letting society go by while concentrating on higher spiritual matters. In responding to Lennon's death by re-creating and romanticizing the spirit and memories of the sixties, some writers seek to celebrate separation from the larger society by reviving the emotions of communitas and re-creating group feelings and identity. They reflect the strong sectarian tendencies of the youth culture (compare Dickstein 1988; McConnell 1987; Tucker 1988), its tendency to draw boundaries between itself and mainstream society. They offer, also, a sense of what is perceived to be lost in the death of Lennon and in the symbolic death of the sixties. Their approach is much like that of a grieving person who denies the death of a loved one, or even a terminally ill person who denies the fact of his own death. Writings in this mode tend to be emotional, almost visceral, in their evocations of a glorious past. These writings turn away from the present and celebrate the old immersion in antistructure.

Turner argues that various propositions are tested in the redressive phase, and these emotional re-creations of the past seem to imply the hope of revival of the old communitas for the group and the possibility of its establishing and maintaining its old sense of difference and separation. This would seem hopeless on any real, material level. It is doubtful anyone really thought a new Haight-Ashbury could spring up or that the nation's campuses would awaken to protest and collective action, but some writings did suggest implicitly that Lennon's death could rekindle collective awareness and action.

Other voices of separation focused on the old shared feelings of anger and opposition. They explored the revival of group solidarity and the possibility of separation in the sharing of various objects of anger. The social stage had changed much since the sixties, though, so new villains were proposed. The most obvious object of collective scorn was Lennon's killer, Mark Chapman, seen as having corrupted counterculture ideals in the same way Chapman himself apparently believed Lennon had corrupted the ideals of innocence and purity portrayed in *The Catcher in the Rye*. Other objects of anger included society, the "Reagan Era," and handguns. To some extent these two strains of separation arguments reflect the two strains of the sixties rebels—the hippie counterculture's penchant for mystic withdrawal and the student New-Left's affinity for confrontational political action. Both voices of separation suggested ways the sixties generation could redefine itself in opposition to the larger society. Writings in the anger mode also reflect the weakness of group identity in 1980, for they did not convincingly construct new "us versus them" contexts, and scapegoating directed at Mark Chapman belied the generation's uncomfortable connections to Lennon's killer

Chapters 5 and 6 consider voices of reintegration, which tend toward two modes as well. One mode of reintegration is surrender. Some elegies argued explicitly or implicitly that the old values were deeply flawed, even invalid, that a terrible mistake had been made, and that the "adults" probably had been right all along. Other voices allowed that the generation's ideals were fine but that we live in a cruel world where goodness cannot survive. Better, then, to let the old ideals die and turn to how to survive in a difficult world that kills dreams and hopes. Communitas was seen as having been false or as having been crushed by the normative weight of structure. These writings suggest a distinct sense of social dislocation among members of the sixties generation, for while they discredit the generation's old ideals, they do not embrace the existing social order. Turner's model does not require a rosy reintegration: In the single most important social drama in U.S. history, the Confederacy sullenly reintegrated in defeat and despair.

Other more numerous writings proposing an active, identity-affirming reintegration may reflect "a yearning for covenant rather than an affirmation of it" (Brueggermann 1977, 272). Nevertheless, they sought to preserve some sense of the group's values and ideals while accepting its place in the social order. These writings reveal how complicated the notion of reintegration is because of the very fragmenting forces of the sixties. Since national cultural values and cultural, social, and political forms had been undercut and deeply questioned, the sixties generation could not easily identify and attach themselves to stable forms. Writers who focused on Lennon's later life, his role as father, and his assertion—made just before his death—that "we must make our own dreams," looked toward ways of reintegration. These voices of reintegration encouraged the sixties generation to reject self-pity and helplessness, to abandon dreams of separation and nostalgic indulgence, and to accept the inevitable processes of life and death, the dialectical inevitability of communitas becoming structure. They reminded the sixties generation (not always gently) that it was time to "grow up" (see, for example, Bangs 1980; Stein 1981).

Some voices of reintegration honored both the dreams of youth and the realities of adulthood, held them simultaneously, and accepted the paradoxical aspects of existence. Writers proposing the reincorporation with society explored possibilities for the construction of a new generational story and an evolving set of meanings pertinent to the personal and collective identities of the sixties people. Reintegration was problematic though, for the social order itself was unstable, and the world of structure that sixties people sought to rejoin was itself in flux.

Chapter 7 focuses on the intensity of generational conflict in 1988. The controversy over Albert Goldman's unflattering biography of Lennon is one sign, among many others, that the social drama for the United States and the internal conflict of the sixties generation have been ongoing throughout the 1980s and that the larger social drama remains in the redressive phase. That Lennon's life and death still could capture public attention as they did in 1988 (a *Newsweek* cover story on October 17), suggests that Lennon indeed remained a focal point in the battle over how a generation wished to view its history.

Chapter 8 returns to the model of social drama as the Lennon controversy swirls out of a generational matrix and becomes more complex and embedded in broader social conflict that takes us to the center of who we are. The "sixties," and by implication the sixties generation, became a broad target for conservative attacks on liberalism in the 1980s. Various generational voices in the mass media suggested a willingness to bend to criticism but also a stubborn refusal to surrender what was left of their sense of generational identity. The level of tension in this and other societal conflicts remains high and indicates that present cultural symbols, categories of identity, and structures of meaning remain deeply conflicted and that new symbols and models for social reconciliation are not yet apparent.

NOTES

1. See Arnold Wolfe (1988) for an analysis of television coverage of Lennon's death.

2. For example, *People* magazine in 1980, appealing to a broad audience, focused on the immediacy of the tragedy for the widow and the child

and on the dangers and problems of celebrity (ironic in a publication that exists to promote and exploit the category of celebrity). The story included long excerpts from a *Playboy* interview with Lennon two months before his death. In that interview, Lennon focused on the present, on where he had arrived at that point in his life; and he looked to the future. While nostalgia in the *People* story was relegated to the many photographs that accompanied the essay, the piece clearly set Lennon in the present and in the mainstream. Titled "In Praise of John Lennon: The Liverpool Lad as Musician, Husband, Father, and Man," its opening paragraph praised Lennon for embarking upon "the most revolutionary undertaking of any rock star's career: an attempt to lead a normal life . . . the last and most meaningful experiment of his life" (27). This "mainstreaming" of Lennon's death did not exclude so much as embrace the sixties generation, and it is part of the reintegrative discourse of acceptance that I discuss later.

Part Two

Voices of Separation

3

Withdrawing to the Past

John Lennon was an important figure for the sixties generation, and his sudden, violent death triggered intense reactions among the segment. The death of an icon who symbolized both its youthful spirit of communitas and its progress toward adulthood impelled the group to reflect on its own identity and its relation to the social order in the context of social dislocation that characterizes social drama. Social dramas move toward reintegration of the social order (always with altered relations and changed terms) or separation of factions through official or tacit agreement. In either case, the particular points of conflict that engendered the drama will have become ameliorated, and ~~passions will~~ have subsided. Many possibilities for both separation and

blic discourse of the redressive phase.
hn Lennon suggest separation, at least
zing memories of communitas and by
r generational anger or scapegoating.
the sixties generation together to cel-
ueness and perhaps to reaffirm former
s turned toward scapegoating and anger
rian tendencies rooted in both the stu-
ure (compare Dickstein 1988; McCon-
ixties youth culture aggressively drew
d what it derisively categorized as
istinctive styles of dress, language, so-
onal and collective relations. It is easy
ment at its well-publicized, highly me-
Trust Anyone Over Thirty." Yet such a
emergence of a new social class—
988; Grossberg 1986; Wiener 1988a)—
ribed patterns of individual identity and

41

The mammoth B

GR .781.66 M

We interrupt th

G 76.195 G 23

I read the New s

78 2.421

relations to society. The cry suggested also that this "class" would not age ideologically; that they could, by virtue of new modes of living and new structures of feeling, always identify with the energy and idealism developed in their chronological youth.

What should be surprising, in retrospect, is not that the sixties generation grew up and assimilated to the adult and straight worlds in various ways, but that so many of its ranks have retained a sense of themselves as "young" for so long (compare Gottlieb 1987; Merser 1987). Perhaps the most significant facet of the sixties generation that justifies it as an object of serious inquiry is its continued sense of identification with the state of youth and the era of the sixties. Numerous writers encouraged such identification in elegies for John Lennon that emphasized the generation's unique experiences and sense of itself, and reflected its problematic identity in 1980.

Emile Durkheim argued that mourning rituals tend to strengthen group solidarity. They provide ways for the social group to reaffirm itself, to establish communion, and to revitalize itself by recalling the past and reviving a sense of social heritage (Alpert 1938, 104–8). Voices of separation focused more on establishing or reviving the old sense of communion and the remembered immersion in liminoid antistructure. Of course, an actual, material separation of this generation from the social order was never likely. Victor Turner emphasizes, however, that in addition to judicial and legislative action, redressive action also is strongly symbolic and ritualistic. In redress, a society and groups that constitute it may "try on" various attitudes and potential solutions, and for powerless and marginalized groups symbolic action may be the only option. In this chapter, I analyze voices of separation that express withdrawal into nostalgia and remembrance of communitas. In the next chapter I analyze voices of separation that engage in scapegoating and anger and revive old antagonisms between the sixties generation and other segments.

One mode of separation offered in writings on Lennon was retreat into memories of the past. Turner posits that the impulse toward meaning in the redressive phase of social drama usually involves contrasting present with past experience and that meaning often emerges from a retrospective framing of the past in light of the present crisis (1985, 217). This retreat to the past in the face of crisis is not uncommon, and researchers on death even suggest it has a positive function (Kubler-Ross 1969; Lifton 1969; Weisman 1972; Wiezman and Kamm 1985).

In its original coining and use in the late seventeenth century, the term "nostalgia" referred to a kind of painful homesickness (Davis 1979, 1–7). In modern usage we tend to equate it also with feelings about the past that are characterized by a sense of longing. Individually we assign different values to these kinds of feelings. In his study of the sociology of nostalgia, Fred Davis (1979) argues that the widespread presence of nostalgia in a society can be a sign of collective and individual identity crises, expressed through a yearning for simpler times. The nostalgia wave in the United States in the 1970s reflected, according to Davis, a form of collective identity crisis largely in response to the cultural and political shocks of the sixties. Nostalgic longing in that period focused on pre-sixties times, mostly the seemingly stable fifties. This pervasive nostalgic impulse of the 1970s may be viewed as part of a redressive period of the social drama precipitated in the sixties. However, the sixties generation seems to have turned *to* the sixties for nostalgia as one way of responding to Lennon's death and as a means of solidifying group consciousness (see Davis 1979, 111–15).

Nostalgia was an easily available, already prevalent, cultural form for responding to a sense of crisis. These nostalgic voices show to some extent how counterculture communitas was remembered and revered in 1980. They show what immediately sprang to mind in considering what was lost and what deserved to be remembered. They retreat from a loss of identity in the present; they pull the group together in an identity-affirming ritual. For writers on Lennon and their audiences, this ritual was one way of turning away from "the cold and nasty sensation of being truly marginal" (Gottlieb 1987, 323). This sense of marginalization included self-doubt about old values and the feeling of being criticized or humored by other segments in the social order.

The question remains—Nostalgia for what? In the context of sixties nostalgia, the particular patterns of thought and feeling that characterized the sense of communitas among the generation, I analyze three elegies that engage and re-create a sense of communitas and reveal perceptions of what has been lost in the passage of time and the altered social order marked by the death of John Lennon. I also consider how some elegies expressed personal nostalgia not connected to the communitas of the sixties generation, thus suggesting the "polysemic" nature of John Lennon as cultural symbol.

THE YOUTH CULTURE: A PAST TO LIVE IN

RECONSTRUCTING COMMUNITAS

In his 1965 novel, *God Bless You Mr. Rosewater*, counterculture literary hero Kurt Vonnegut describes a future so mechanized that almost everyone is unemployed. The government, reflecting the epitome of bureaucratic concern, has opened free suicide centers. A man enters one of the centers, and as he is being strapped into a chair to receive his lethal injection, the nurse mentions something about God. The man turns to the nurse and says, matter of factly, "There is one question I *would* like to ask God—Just what in hell are people *for?*"

The sixties generation asked the same question. It valued human interaction as an end in itself and challenged what it saw as a rationalized and bureaucratized society that seemed to encourage a mechanistic, utilitarian individualism. Much of the mourning for Lennon in 1980 invoked this fundamental tenet of sixties communitas: "In the plurality of freedom, we become slave of the master: Solitude. We each wage our battles by ourselves, for ourselves and/or our families. After all, that's the American way, isn't it?" (Wiegand 1980). Rolf Wiegand, a columnist for the *Cincinnati Enquirer*, describes the individualist tradition and its seeming intensification as the Reagan Era begins. In 1980, according to Wiegand, Americans feel their burdens harshly because "there is no unity, no communion in that experience." But in Lennon's death we are reminded of his message of "*communion* over the freedom of the individual enshrined in the foundation of American institutions" (B4).

Describing the sixties as a shared chapter of our lives, *Christian Science Monitor* staff writer Christopher Swan (1980, 7) remembers the Beatles as "our friends, our fellow voyagers, our magic selves." Swan focuses on the public nature of the Beatles' music, how in 1969 strains of the newly released *Abbey Road* "thundered out into the night, echoing through the dark streets. You could just feel the energy of happiness . . . reverberating through the night."

In the wake of Lennon's death, writers rekindled the old communitas. Almost magically, remembers Pete Hamill in a long feature piece on Lennon in *New York* magazine (1980), "people just seemed to appear" outside the Dakota apartments within hours of Lennon's death. Hamill sees the mourners as special people, "not the people you see at plane crashes or at great fires, the injured geeks of the dangerous city. These were people who might come together to mourn the smashing of a work of art." He depicts the scene reverently. The mourners gathered, says Hamill, "to express silent witness." As they sing "Give Peace a Chance," Hamill reminisces about the old communion when he heard 500,000 people sing Lennon's words during an antiwar moratorium. By the next morning, observes Hamill, "the gates of the Dakota looked like the wall of a Mexican church, or an instant Lourdes, covered with a collage of flowers, messages, photographs, drawings." The gates took on the aura of a "new Holy Place" (39).

What was shared, what was holy, these writers suggest, was truth itself. The music that fueled the sixties communitas, wrote G. G. Murray in a letter to the *Boston Globe*, impelled "seismic rumblings of change" that induced visionary pilgrimages. "Millions heard the call—and left all to follow—not the Beatles, but those chords that had been struck and sounded within each of us. A world in change required a new kind of courage—to seek and find that which is absolute, that changes not in the face of human turmoil" (Murray 1980, 12).

Recurring words in these passages such as *journey, pilgrimage, truth, search, witness, vision,* and *dream* suggest religious overtones and reflect the deep, mystical side of communitas in their celebration of a religious type of communion. In the specific context of 1980, what was revived was the sense of sharing a deep, essential truth, and this situation suggests a certain irony. As the sixties generation lived through the 1970s and into the 1980s, it found itself increasingly immersed in the structural forms of the mainstream culture it had rejected, most obviously in the forms of work and family. The free-floating sixties communitas is celebrated as a source of solace, as a kind of spiritual and emotional home lost in the structure and individualism of 1980. As Turner emphasizes, communitas, to be effective, must be transitory, must finally be reintegrative. The energy of sixties communitas did not easily foster such reintegrative with a fragmented society. Though some sixties people had turned to specific structural movements in the 1970s such as evangelical Christianity, Eastern religion, and the human potential movement, most simply had drifted back into extant social and cultural forms, "restrained from [the] quest for community, and severed from [the] aim of overturning the established order," and become confused about their moral and ethical approaches to life (Tipton 1982, 30). The nostalgic mode briefly celebrated a segment's lost faith, a faith that apparently had not been replaced with anything of comparable power.

COUNTERCULTURE ETHOS

Turner's generalizations about hippie communitas (1969, 1974) have been expanded empirically in the work of Steven Tipton (1982).[1] Tipton describes the communitas of the sixties generation as a critical response to two older "styles of ethical evaluation": (a) an authoritarian Bible-based religion/cultural system that valued obedience, duty, and structural communities dedicated to moral ends, and (b) utilitarian individualism, a consequential ethical style that valorized efficient designation of wants and the means to obtain them. Handmaiden to modernity, utilitarian individualism relied on the conditions of the market economy and bureaucratic social organization. It emphasized utility rather than duties, and it privatized the older, biblical, holy community. At the time of the emergence of the counterculture, American mainstream culture already reflected a fairly long history of functioning in the utilitarian mode but celebrating itself in the biblical mode. The 1960s opened with such an act, as John F. Kennedy preached, "Ask not what your country can do for you. . . ."

The sixties youth culture rejected both the authoritarian biblical mode, with its enforced and constricting demands on community, and the utilitarian mode, with its rampant, seemingly directionless individualism. It developed a monistic ethos that posited an ultimate cosmic reality. This reality was realized individually by exploring the inner self. Communion was established among those who had followed that path. The means of reaching this state included psychedelic drugs, music, and meditation. Although the word "community" was used often by sixties people, what they celebrated was not the highly structured, taken-for-granted inhibitions of physical community but rather the emotional sharing of communion.[2] Turner observed that the hippies felt united in a common experience, which began with the exploration of the self and noted that such conditions characterize the state of communitas where personal identities are not merged but take on likeness in their shared liberation from conformity to general norms (1974, 274). Communitas may be expressed simultaneously as group feeling and individual expression.

NOSTALGIC ELEGIES

Voices of nostalgia, ranging in form from letters to the editor to long feature essays, appeared in various publications such as the *Boston Globe,* the *Cincinnati Enquirer, Christian Science Monitor, New York* magazine, *Rolling Stone,* and *Newsweek.* I analyze three longer elegies that reflect an immersion in the supposed glories of the past: Scott Spencer's elegy in *Rolling Stone*, "John Lennon" (1981); Jack Kroll's feature piece in *Newsweek,* "Strawberry Fields Forever" (1980); and Ken Kesey's long remembrance in *Rolling Stone,* "On the Passing of John Lennon" (1981). Spencer's and Kroll's elegies provide insights into significant aspects of counterculture communitas—the complex relationship between the individual and the group and the

romantic roots of the counterculture ethos. Kesey's piece both celebrates and problematizes the old communitas and offers a transition
to subsequent chapters, which analyze the voices of reintegration.
These elegies focus on re-creating central tenets of counterculture
thought and feeling and turn away implicitly from generational problems in 1980 of identity and social placement.

MYSTICAL UNION WITH JOHN LENNON

Scott Spencer's 1,000-word piece, "John Lennon," appeared in the
January 22, 1981, issue of *Rolling Stone* (13), which was devoted almost exclusively to the memory of John Lennon. Spencer begins by
reflecting on the incomprehensiblity of Lennon's death, which is
"dispiriting." Spencer says that everything he sees reminds him of death
and reflects on his childhood and how he and his friends so often
played at dying: "Half the games we played as children were about
killing each other. . . . we were trying to learn the art of dying while
we were still rightfully stupid enough to bear it." The key word for
Spencer is art. For he elegizes Lennon as, above all, a great artist
who taught many things, not the least of which was how to die. Spencer mentions news reports that as Lennon lay bleeding to death in the
police car that rushed him to the hospital, his last word was, "Yeah."
Spencer finds an affirmation in that last word and posits that "we,"
all who mourn Lennon, knew "everything Lennon meant" because
Lennon achieved a supreme artistic form of communication.

Spencer emphasizes Lennon's genius as an example of the power
of art and uses traditional terminology in forging what appears to be
a traditional argument about art's power, but in asserting that members of the sixties generation knew Lennon in a special way, Spencer
goes beyond the bounds of traditional aesthetic arguments:

> Because he allowed us to know him, John Lennon gave us the chance
> to share his death, to resume the preparation for our own. Because we
> were so used to the way he thought, the habits, the turns, the surprises
> of his mind, we can enter him as we remember his last moments, to let
> it be us in the car, pulling up to the curb, opening the door, stepping
> out, breathing the night. Someone said he was happy that night and we
> somehow know what his happiness felt like, and we can imagine our-
> selves resurgent, electric with energy. (13)

Spencer works several central counterculture concerns. The notion
that Lennon's death might help us prepare for our own, for example,

reflects the influence of Eastern religion and its particular importance to the LSD experience for early users, who often approached LSD use in a religious and philosophical spirit, as a death and rebirth experience in which the ego is sacrificed to permit the birth of the truer inner self. The Tibetan Book of the Dead was used often as a preparatory manual for first-time LSD users (see Gottlieb 1987, 175; Stevens 1988, 50; Tipton 1982, 121–24). The statement also is ironic. If Lennon's death does signal the death of the sixties, the death of the old communitas, it reminds us also that we, too, will die physically in the present and future worlds of structure and struggle. The statement hints at the discourse of acceptance and reintegration.

The primary focus of the passage, though, is on sixties communitas, as Spencer evokes a sense of total union with the artist not through a work of art (aesthetics) but through a direct, seemingly unmediated merging (mysticism). Embedded in the traditional language and appeal to the power of art lies a monism that "makes one's innermost feelings ultimately integral with those of others and with the transpersonal nature of the universe" (Tipton, 16). This mystical union, which allows Spencer to leapfrog the mediation of art and to inhabit Lennon, to "be" him, blurs distinctions between the personal and the collective; Spencer calls it "the moral transparency of genius" through which Lennon could "create a community of hearts and minds from 10 million separate appetites." Spencer evokes the old feelings of communion: "Part of the grief we feel about his murder is our longing to once more belong to something larger than ourselves, to feel our heart beat in absolute synchrony with hearts everywhere." This longing has been assuaged momentarily in the "unifying force" of Lennon's death.

Spencer shifts, in his conclusion, to the personal level, claiming that Lennon set an example for our own individual strivings: "He proved that you could follow your vision, explore your talents, speak your mind—take any leap you dare. In a cautious age John Lennon was uninterested in existing on any but his own terms." Steeped in romantic notions of the power of art and in similar romantic contradictions between the primacy of social unity and individuality, Spencer's elegy presents Lennon simultaneously as a symbol of mystical union and individualism. This yoking is warranted by his (and presumably our) mystical union with Lennon the unique individual, which in the context of sixties communitas is the very foundation of community.

This central counterculture notion of individual and group as function of each other was expressed in passing by other writers. In *Roll-*

ing Stone, Greil Marcus wrote, "The Beatles and their fans played out an image of utopia, of a good life, and the image was that one could join a group and by doing so not lose one's identity but find it: find one's own voice" (1981, 26). Marcus, expressing the counterculture notion of an ideal, intersubjective reality reached via getting in touch with oneself (see Tipton 1982, 19), posits that our reasons for caring about John Lennon are fundamentally the same, which enables him to say, "It was other people's reactions to John Lennon's murder that produced in me the most overwhelming despair" (Marcus, 27). In a similar vein, Todd Gitlin wrote in *Center Magazine*, "The Beatles proved that you did not have to lose your individuality when you entered a group or a movement. In fact their collaboration made each individual shine all the more distinctly" (1981, 3). "That these were Beatles songs, not the single expression of an individual, needs to be remembered amid all the Lennon eulogies, which call him the strong creative force of the group," cautioned Jay Cocks in *Time* magazine (1980, 24). John Leonard, in the *New York Times*, said of the Beatles, "They could, in their marvelous music, move from a self in isolation to an ideal community, and we did expect them to be that self-ratifying community forever. They refused" (1980, 30).

SIXTIES YOUTH AND THE CHILD IN ROMANTICISM

Born of an educated middle class, the sixties counterculture borrowed freely from nineteenth-century romanticism in constructing its ethos and in its choice of symbols and metaphors (see for example, Gouldner 1971, 78–80; Musgrove 1974, 65–80; Roszak 1969, 239–68). As John Spencer elegizes Lennon in the romantic tradition of the special power of the artist, adding elements of mystical communion, so Jack Kroll, in a four-page feature piece in the December 22, 1980, edition of *Newsweek*, evokes traditional romantic notions of the special acumen of childhood and the concomitant loss of innocence and utopian vision, though he makes no specific reference to romantic traditions. Kroll opens by quoting a blurb that John Lennon wrote for a Liverpool pop music magazine in 1961. In that piece Lennon described the origin of the Beatles in a parody of scripture: "Still there was no beat and a kindly old aged man said, quote 'Thou hast not drums!'" Kroll sees Lennon's piece as "a child's scripture announcing a children's revolution" (41).

Ostensibly tracing the development and subsequent loss of the

Wordsworthian "visionary gleam" and echoing William Blake's *Songs of Innocence*, Kroll places Lennon as the leader of a revolution in which "the center of creative consciousness shifted to young people" (41). Kroll focuses on the romantic theme of child prescience by quoting Lennon's statement that he had visions as a child and thought he "must be a genius but nobody's noticed" (41). Kroll characterizes the sixties communitas that the Beatles ruled over as "the new techno-pop tribalism," echoing the terminology of Marshall McLuhan, a patron saint of many of the sixties generation largely because his metaphor of the "global village" suggested such a techno-tribalism based on shared mass-mediated experiences. Kroll assuages the group's self-doubts about their old communitas by arguing that the children's revolution "was not self-indulgence, it was the central energy of civilized people" (41). The children rebelled against the "sick, mean-spirited" hells of the grownups with "a popular ecstasy, a joyful noise, a creative elation," all led by "the Beatles and their poet-comedian, John Lennon." Kroll's words and style ring with the biblical language of Blake and provide a tone suitable for group affirmation characteristic of mourning rituals. Kroll suggests the shaman in Lennon also:

> And the songs did heal: good music is instant evolution; it changes your breathing, the way you focus your eyes at the world, it shifts the rhythm of your thinking, hoping, fearing. It dances your mind into places where its ordinary processes, however subtle, would never take you. (42)

For all of Lennon's individual genius, Kroll sees Lennon's best work as having been done when Lennon was the central head of a "four-headed Orpheus" (42). To locate Lennon's genius in the context of the Beatles is to locate it in the sixties. But with Lennon the idea of the Beatles died, too. What is left then is an aching, romantic sense of lost childhood, lost utopia. Kroll concludes his elegy with reference to two Beatles masterpieces, Paul McCartney's "Penny Lane" and Lennon's "Strawberry Fields." They are great songs, says Kroll, because they reflect Lennon's and McCartney's "genius at blending images of utopia and loss, a beautiful but tough idealism about reality and its way of dissolving into dream" (44). In Kroll's celebration, the "trumpet-tongued nostalgia" of "Penny Lane" and the "lost utopia of childhood" in "Strawberry Fields" fall like ferns in the sedimentation of memory. Lennon's and McCartney's memories become our memories of both a time in history and our own personal times, our own youths. To situate the memory of Lennon in this Wordsworthian way, is to end in aching nostalgia, for to enter the world "trailing clouds of glory" is to reduce the rest of life to nostalgia or tedium. Indeed to remember sixties communitas in this romantic vein is to render the present pale and unsatisfying and provides a key to understanding how many of those who gathered together for collective mourning used the sad occasion to create the feeling of that lost utopia of childhood.

The force of Kroll's piece lies in his intense evocation of sixties communitas, in his focus on Lennon as Beatle and as leader of a children's revolution. Late in the essay, Kroll mentions Lennon's relationship with Yoko Ono briefly and allows that she "answered some deep need in his sensibility." But Kroll quickly shifts Lennon's meaning back into the nostalgic context: "But whatever the future might have brought with Yoko, it seems clear that Lennon's best work is locked up in the magic circle of the '60s." The focus clearly is on the past, on what has been lost, not what might have been for Lennon or on what might be for the sixties generation.

LENNON AS MARKER FOR PERSONAL MEMORIES

The suggestion in Kroll's elegy of the blending of personal and collective memory is an appropriate signal for considering that not all nostalgia necessarily reflected generational grieving for lost communitas. The generational theme of the loss of the sixties did not own Lennon and could not contain all cultural meaning. Lennon was mourned and remembered also in the context of the larger society. Some of that remembrance was nostalgic, but it marked personal time and situated the self in progress through life. These ways of remembering are developmental and reflect an accommodation to structure and the accepted forms, such as having children and growing old, that mark the passing of time.

Simon Frith (1984) has argued that the idea of a "rock movement" in the sixties, a notion central to the counterculture elegies I analyze in this chapter, was an illusion because the music's production and reception always have been deeply embedded in economic structures; rock music is capitalist to its core. What force and importance rock music does have lie in the realm of "transitory private pleasures." The following nostalgic pieces do focus on those private memories and feelings that Frith suggests are the site of meaning for rock music. However, they also are the work of "primary definer" journalists, as are the antistructure essays. As such, they suggest collective voices proposing ways that "we" remember.

These "in-structure" pieces on Lennon that do not express counterculture memories are examples of what John Fiske (1986, 1989) calls "polysemic popular texts." These texts have many seams, or potential openings. On one level, popular texts assume a passive audience, are easily accessible, and require little work of the reader. Popular texts are produced from ideological standpoints and are most easily read or experienced within that embrace, but in order to be popular, Fiske argues, these texts must appeal to huge numbers of people positioned across different segments. Meaning in popular texts must be fluid and allow room for various readings of people postioned differently in the social matrix. John Lennon seemed not to seek widespread popularity; nevertheless, the sheer power, and perhaps genius, of his songwriting and performing gained him that popularity. His songs and his persona could have attained such popularity, according to Fiske, only if they were polysemic and allowed for multiple meanings. The "text" of John Lennon was open and available beyond the sixties generation and could be for many "a cultural resource to think through their social experience" (Fiske 1989, 30).

Many writers recounted how Beatles music and Beatlemania had marked their childhood, adolescence, and youth. Women recalled their teen and preteen crushes and the endless discussions of who was their favorite Beatle. Men remembered growing their hair longer and feeling rebellious, perhaps for the first time. Such accounts often included specific references to songs—dancing that first close dance to "If I Fell," cruising Main Street to "Twist and Shout," or moodily shuffling down dark streets to the strains of "Eleanor Rigby" (see, for example, "Growing up with the Beatles," 1980; "*Washington Post* reporters discuss . . . ," 1980).

One such reminiscence, by Billy Reed in the *Louisville Courier-Journal*, is representative of personal rather than generational remembrance:

> The news of John Lennon's death made me think of people and times that I hadn't thought about for awhile. It took me back to college and to lots of soft, lazy afternoons that stretched into hard days' nights.
> If you're around my age, which is 37, you can't think of the 1960s without thinking of the Beatles. They were always there, in the background. We let them hold our hands. We let them take us on a magical mystery tour of our time. (1980, E7)

Reed recounts when he first heard of the Beatles (from "a girl in Danville") and the night he heard their first album at a college dance. He remembers that rock and roll had "flattened out" in the early 1960s and that the Beatles were "the Next Step." He resurrects clichéd observations—"The girls all liked Paul McCartney . . . John was the intellectual." In contrast to the counterculture elegies, Reed separates Lennon and the Beatles from the turmoil of the sixties (E7):

> The Beatles brought some fun into college in the mid-1960s and, heavens, we needed some. Things were starting to get real serious back then. We had already lost Kennedy. The ghettos were smoldering. And there was a war growing in some place called Vietnam. But if you were a college student in Lexington, Ky., or anywhere else for that matter, you could escape all that, not to mention term papers and exams, by slipping off to some place like the Green Lantern or Adams or the Buffalo Tavern and putting some Beatles on the jukebox.

Reed's sixties differ markedly from Kroll's "children's revolution." Lennon, rather than being a mystical partner we could enter (as in Spencer's elegy), is a disembodied voice providing the soundtrack over a reel of personal memories. For Reed, Lennon and the Beatles signify escape from the turmoil of the political and personal worlds, and his casual linking of smoldering ghettos and term papers as irritants has the sting of truth in depicting the actual day-to-day lived experience of college students, radical and conservative, during the sixties. Reed appropriates Lennon, the Beatles, and the 1960s into his own history where they serve as markers in his personal narrative. In 1980, Lennon's death becomes a sign for aging, as Reed notes that he has to explain who the Beatles were to a daughter born in 1972. He wonders if his friends from college felt "as sad and old and vulnerable" as he.

Lennon serves as a conventional marker for Reed, just as images and memories of Frank Sinatra or John Wayne might mark the lives of an earlier generation. One major difference between Reed's account and "death of the sixties" accounts is that Reed does not invest his Lennon, the sixties, or the Beatles with special historical or transcendental significance in claiming that Beatles music served a common quest for absolute truth. There is no sense in Reed's comments on Lennon that his own youth experience has been substantively different from preceding or succeeding youth experiences. Reed's account stands, I propose, as a fairly typical example of a mass-mediated relationship with Lennon and a lived experience of the sixties absent feelings of communitas. Reed views Lennon from within the framework of structure, even from the remembered perspective of youth.[3]

Such "in-structure" remembrances of Lennon include memories of members of older generations. Al Harting of the *Dallas Morning News* (1980) sadly recalled how he denied his sons, then aged 14 and 11, permission to see the Beatles' live performance in Dallas in 1964. As publicity director for the charter air service flying the Beatles on part of their U.S. tour, Harting had seen enough of Beatlemania to fear for his young sons' safety at the concert. He did allow his sons to go with him to meet the Beatles at the airport. As Lennon stepped off the plane and onto the metal ramp, two small hands grabbed his ankle. They belonged to Harting's eleven-year-old son, Bert, who "compelled by a force he couldn't resist . . . settled for snaring any of the Beatles but John was the closest." Harting remembers Lennon's measured response, "Turn me loose, mate," he glowered. Harting did manage to get his boys some towels the Beatles had used at the Muehlenbach Hotel in Kansas City. He concludes:

> The boys are grown and gone now, but they left me with the towels. I took them out of the box and looked at them again the day John Lennon died, and remembered with a guilty lump in my throat, how Bert had clung to John Lennon's ankle when John, Paul, George and Ringo came to see us on that day 16 years ago out at Love Field. (7C)

Lennon's memory is appropriated directly in the service of structure, as a poignant moment when a father reflects on an important event in the history of his relationship with his sons.

Personal memories of Lennon and the Beatles served even more conservative ends. A *Dallas Morning News* piece (Schwartz 1980, 1C) focused on a fifty-seven-year-old woman who felt saddened by Lennon's death because, as she watched television biographies after his death, she remembered that "sweet-faced young man in a suit and tie . . . [who looked] like what I would now call clean cut, all-American." Like some parents of teens in the 1960s, she forbade her daughter to play Beatles music and was "horrified" and "disgusted" by their assault on traditional values. But the television images of Lennon as early Beatle stood out for her in contrast to the ensuing years of hippies and drugs. That fresh-faced young Lennon seemed tame compared to what followed: "a group naming itself the Grateful Dead, musicians destroying their instruments on stage, singers sticking safety pins in their cheeks." Lennon's memory, in this case, is associated with the pre-hippie 1960s; he and the early Beatle era are recalled with fondness as symbols of innocence before the terrible dislocations later in the 1960s and 1970s.

These three samples of nostalgia reduce Lennon to a supporting role in a larger story of personal lives in a structured, though troubled, world of ongoing sequential events. The last piece suggests also the context of the social drama begun in the 1960s, as Lennon is reconstructed selectively to stand symbolically in opposition to the very feelings and events held sacred in the sixties generation's nostalgic elegies. These voices of structure provide a useful backdrop for considering Ken Kesey's nostalgic elegy, which is more cautiously celebratory of counterculture communitas.

The nostalgic impulse as reflected in the counterculture elegies is celebratory. Yet we see in it also the barest ripples of contradiction and conflict. The inherent romanticism of sixties communitas reflects strains between the personal and the collective, validating both without clearly establishing a baseline that balances freedom and responsibility. Injunctions to "do your own thing" and "love thy neighbor" inevitably collide outside the liminoid forms of communitas. The last-passages of Jack Kroll's elegy suggest that the nostalgia for lost childhood is personal as well as collective and that Lennon's and the Beatles' music always held that contradiction. It also hints at the truth that individuals, including many in this generational segment, who form their identities in the adulation of youth itself, consequently have difficulty defining themselves as adults.

KEN KESEY'S RELUCTANT NOSTALGIA

Ken Kesey's long elegy for Lennon in the March 5, 1981, edition of *Rolling Stone* reflects elements of both nostalgia and resignation. It is centered around three parables about three visitors to his farm around the time of Lennon's death. The first short parable is about Bible Bill, a drunk who seeks to exploit Kesey's celebrity status by leading a group of only semi-interested teenagers to Kesey's door to show them he knows the great writer. The shortest and least developed of the three parables, its purpose seems to be to highlight the irritations of celebrity. The second tells of the visit of an old hippie, John the Groupie, who is with the Kesey family as they hear of Lennon's death. The third parable describes a visit by an angry, confused young man of this post-sixties era, Patrick the Punk. Kesey's accounts probably are only loosely based in actual events.

The section on John the Groupie, though celebratory, reveals tension between structure and antistructure; it is a piece both warm with feeling and cold with foreboding, poised on the edge of 1980, in Kesey's words, "the Chilly Season of Reagan." The piece opens and closes on the subject of Lennon's courage. Kesey relates a scene at the Apple recording studios in London at Christmastime, 1968, when Lennon stopped an incipient brawl between some Apple executives and a couple of Hell's Angels who were Kesey's traveling companions. As both sides poised for battle, Kesey remembers Lennon strolling into the room dressed in a Santa Claus suit: "Awright then; that's enough," Lennon said firmly. And it was: "He was something," says Kesey. "When he said 'Peace,' even the warring Angels listened" (24).

Though he playfully invests the scene with a mock-heroic grandeur, Kesey also celebrates Lennon as a symbol of sixties communitas, as the very incarnation of its central premise of "peace." The scene evokes memories of the power of a communitas that was so strong it even briefly domesticated the Hell's Angels, and it reminds of the fashionable romanticizing of outlaw figures and aestheticizing of violence in sixties popular culture, for example in *Bonnie and Clyde* and *Butch Cassidy and the Sundance Kid* (see Gitlin 1980, 197–202). If society was sick at its core, sixties rebels deduced that there must be something good in its outlaws and outcasts. Such assumptions sometimes proved dangerous to naive middle-class kids (see Lukas 1987, 339–60). Still, Kesey was himself one of the major players in the attempt to convert the Angels to more peaceful pursuits via LSD (Stevens 1988, 221–44 and 323–25). Less than one year after the Apple studio episode, at the infamous Altamont concert in northern California, Hell's Angels, hired ostensibly for crowd control, stabbed a man to death a few feet in front of the stage as the Rolling Stones sang "Sympathy for the Devil."

A successful novelist, counterculture hero, and subject of well-known stories, Kesey had "retired" to a farm in Oregon in the 1970s. Steeped in traditional structural forms such as family, land, livestock, and crops, he grapples with both personal and cultural contradictions in this elegy for Lennon, wavering between a stern code that at times resembles American frontier individualism and a sense of social responsibility and fidelity to counterculture values.[4] For example, the whole Kesey family, it seems, has a weakness for picking up and taking in strangers. On the day of Lennon's death, Kesey relates that he and his daughter returned to the house after mending fences in bitterly cold weather to find John the Groupie warming his hands above the stove. "About thirty-five or forty, with a lot of hard mileage in his eyes" (25), John has ended up at the Kesey place pretty much by accident. He caught a ride out of L.A. going to Orgeon and, well, this is Oregon.

Kesey is angered by the intrusion and by what John represents— that looney, irresponsible end of the counterculture spectrum. Kesey, in the role of practical farmer, is especially angered that this person shows up in subfreezing weather dressed in sneakers and a short-sleeved shirt. But Kesey can't stay mad at him, allowing that John the Groupie is "likable—just your basic stringy, carrot-topped, still-down-and-it-looks-up-to-me acid head flowerchild gone to seed. Probably no dope he hasn't tried and, what's more, none he wouldn't try again. Still grooving, still tripping, he didn't give a shit if he was barefoot in a blizzard" (25). Kesey tells John sternly that he can spend the night out in the guest cabin, adding quickly that he will be driven to Interstate 5 first thing in the morning.

After dark, John the Groupie wanders back up to the house. Kesey's boys had shot ducks the day before; leftovers lay on the table. One of the children had set a place at the table for the bedraggled stranger. The family gathers in the warmth on the far end of the room. While feeding the stranger, the Kesey family directs their attention not to Bible reading, storytelling, cooperative crafts, or even Zen chanting, but to *Monday Night Football*. Kesey sneaks glances at the strange visitor, who "ate the carcasses so clean that red ants wouldn't have bothered over the leavings." The visitor also ate a whole loaf of bread and "a pot of rice big enough for a family of Cambodian refugees." John the Groupie is shown to be a kind of perfected counterculture type who has withstood the test of time. Animal-like (in a Disney sense), immersed in a devil-may-care existence of tripping and direct experience, "he ate slowly and with bemused determination, not like a glutton eats, but like a coyote who never knows how long it might be before the next feast so he better get it all down" (24). Kesey begrudgingly appreciates this economy of survival, this frail but persistent—like the coyote—relic of a lost time. Kesey says he kept his eyes on the football game, "not wanting to embarrass him by letting on" he was watching.

Then, Howard Cosell's voice tells them all that John Lennon has been shot and killed outside his apartment in New York:

> I turned to see if John the Groupie had heard the news. He had. He was twisted toward me in his seat, his mouth open, the last duck carcass stopped midway between tooth and table. We looked into each other's eyes across the room. Our roles fell away. No more scowling landowner and ingratiating tramp, but simply old allies, united in sudden hurt by the news of a mutual hero's death. We could have held each other and wept. (25)

The next day, John the Groupie gets a ride right away on Interstate 5. Over the radio Kesey hears that "everybody was picking up everybody today, everywhere" (67). The moral of the visitation of John the Groupie is simple, says Kesey: *"Don't forget the Magical Summer of Love in the Chilly Season of Reagan"* (68).

Clearly, Kesey shows Lennon's death to have a brief unifying effect based on shared experiences, on a brief glimmer of the old communitas. Though the story sets Kesey against John the Groupie, sets the present against the past, and sets structure against antistructure, Kesey moves in steps toward a sense of communion with John. Initially irritated, he acknowledges begrudging acceptance, even admiration, for John as a relic and ends with a brief moment of kinship, "united in sudden hurt by the news of a mutal hero's death." And the task of letting John go, of dropping him off on the highway, is made easier by the brief flowering of communitas, since "everybody was picking up everybody today, everywhere." He ends this part of the essay by setting the image of the apex of the counterculture, the 1967 Summer of Love in northern California, as an ideal past in contrast to the present—the Chilly Season of Reagan.

Kesey prepares the reader for Lennon's unifying force in his opening story, which shows Lennon as the bringer, indeed the enforcer, of peace. It seem appropriate, in retrospect, that Lennon assumes this role in the guise of Santa Claus, the bringer of gifts to children, and not Jesus, the symbol of eternal life attained only through suffering and death. The symbolism hints at the indulgent, self-absorbed, and child-like nature of counterculture values, experience, politics, and world view. Wary of celebrating such a past, Kesey seems to circle it, poking in a finger here, dipping in a toe there. He sets himself against John the Groupie in the opening and is moved only briefly to the old feelings of communion. The past and present seem at odds in Kesey, and as I will show in a later chapter, he concludes his elegy for Lennon by undercutting the joy of communitas and turning toward a somewhat depressive assessment of the legacy of the counterculture past.

1980: AMERICA AND THE IDEAL PAST

These nostalgic re-creations of counterculture communitas reflect a turning away from the present reality implied by the death of the sixties. The focus of these elegies is on good memories of the past, and that should provide clues as to how the past is felt and reconstructed, just what about the sixties is valued in 1980. That these elegies focus on the counterculture suggests, I believe, that it was those values and feelings that the sixties generation had called most into question by 1980. To retreat into them was to indicate, implicitly, that counterculture values had become problematic or even that they had been lost. But these elegies also may reflect a last attempt to celebrate and perhaps revitalize the old feelings, to give them life or credence once more. In that sense they do appear to function, as Durkheim believed death rituals function, to strengthen group solidarity by reaffirming shared values and reviving the social heritage of a segment. Ironically, just as Ronald Reagan was symbolizing a reaffirmation of older mainstream values (as evidenced in the Dallas woman's remembrance of a sweet, safe John Lennon), voices of the sixties counterculture reaffirmed the "old" values for their segment also. In 1980, both the mainstream culture and the counterculture retreated to nostalgia for an idealized past, a situation that suggests feelings of anxiety about the present (see Davis 1977).

The pervasiveness of this sense of uneasiness that signals problems in the meaning system of the social order and seems to breed nostalgia is evident in "mainstream" discourse such as Theodore White's account of the 1980 presidential campaign. White had planned for the 1980 presidential election to be the last he would cover for his *Making of the President* series of books, which began with the 1960 Kennedy–Nixon campaign. His final book in the series would include the 1980 campaign and a summing up of the campaigns he had covered during the preceding twenty years, but in his preface to *America in Search of Itself* (1982), White expresses doubt that he could show just where the nation had come to in 1980. He sees a country that had "lost its way" (1). The story of 1980, White believes, had to begin with postwar America and the "intoxication of victory" that lasted a generation (3). The story was being closed, though, with a picture of "a humiliated nation with a sense of victory squandered, searching itself and its way, questioning its beliefs because the old ideas did not stretch to cover present reality" (5).

No doubt, White argues, this questioning process had begun in the sixties, which "opened an age of experiment, and age of hope . . . with a sense of total unlimited power to do the nation's will at home and abroad" (5). White offers a mainstream view of "the death of the sixties" as the demise of postwar liberalism (see also Matusow 1984) In White's view, one of the great paradoxes of the sixties was that its impetus for increased individual rights resulted in increased government controls. Consequently, part of the reaction of 1980 had to do with the "consequence and reach of government, . . . the murky limits that separate the public interest from individual rights" (7). It is easy to forget that the sixties counterculture rebelled against a nation of "liberals" who had elected Lyndon Johnson in a landslide.

In his conclusion, White senses that the election of 1980 has left the nation in an unresolved state:

I write and close this book in a clouded time, not knowing whether it is twilight or dawn, an era ending or an era beginning. Future historians will find the Reagan experiment a fascinating study as it approaches its climax. But this drama is for the politicians of today to manage. (433)

White here expresses a fundamental aspect of the redressive phase of social drama, a sense that meaning and purpose in a society are problematic and that the collective "we" cannot be sure of who and where they are; in this particular instance, whether Reagan's election portends a new order or is merely symptomatic of the present disorder. In 1980, apparently many Americans across many segmental lines faced a troubled present and could imagine only an uncertain future. Understandably, they were prone to take refuge in the past.

For some elegists, remembering John Lennon meant taking refuge in the memories of communitas, withdrawing into the past, and rekindling old feelings that set the sixties generation apart from the rest of society. Others attempted to identify collective foes and rekindle old feelings of shared enmity.

NOTES

1. In *Getting Saved from the Sixties* (1982), Tipton argues that sixties counterculture youth joined alternative religious movements in the 1970s in order to make moral sense of their lives. Tipton's study is the result of seven years (1972–79) of fieldwork among members of Christian, Zen Buddhist, and human potential movement communities. Fieldwork included taped formal interviews, surveys, and participant observation for the purposes of describing the search for moral values. Although much has been written about the social and cultural movements of the sixties, Tipton's deep and rich research produces the clearest and most data-based description of counterculture values.

2. See Schmalenbach (1961) for important distinctions between community and communion. Community, according to Schmalenbach, is structured and taken for granted, based on spatial and temporal contiguity (332); for example, the rural village and the nuclear and extended family. Community is generally outside the range of emotion. Feelings play little part in community: "neighbors and brothers always remain neighbors and brothers" (335). Communion, on the other hand, is shared emotional experience. In the emotional experience of communion, people discover a sense of belonging to a "new" category. Schmalenbach argues that the contemporary yearning for community among the educated reflects a romantic confusion of community and communion (332). Especially relevant to the sixties counterculture are

Schmalenbach's observations that those who are not members of a community are attracted to the social elements of a community that suggest communion and that those yearning for community are often sensitive, emotionally differentiated people who probably would not be able to live in structural communities (338). An excellent account of the trials of a sixties counterculture type attempting to reenter her old worlds of family and geographic community is Blanche McCrary Boyd's *The Redneck Way of Knowledge* (1982).

3. A similar piece is *Los Angeles Times* writer Kathleen Hendrix's remembrance (1980) of how intensely the Beatles influenced youngsters she was teaching in Borneo in 1964 as a Peace Corps volunteer. She says she feared the Beatles would take over their local culture, but when she returned in 1976 she found her old students playing traditional instruments and music: "This is not to say rock 'n' roll had disappeared. It was entrenched. But we had incorporated the Beatles, and each other, and had moved on."

4. Kesey's best known novels, *One Flew Over the Cuckoo's Nest* and *Sometimes a Great Notion,* strongly take the side of the individual against society. Yet during his days as counterculture guru in the late sixties, he searched constantly for what he called the experience of "group mind," the blending of separate individuals into one consciousness (Stevens 1988, 234).

4

Scapegoating and Anger

Other voices of separation suggested a rekindling of the old shared feelings of anger and opposition, a continuance of the ritual solidification of group awareness, and a reviving of the "us versus them" divisions of the sixties. This impulse toward separation celebrates shared antagonisms, while the nostalgic impulse celebrates shared feelings and values. John Fiske notes (1989, 24) that social allegiances formed in and around popular culture often reflect shared enmity, a sense of a common enemy. To be against the war in Vietnam, against racism, against drug laws, and against repression in the sixties was usually an initial step to sharing in group consciousness and communion. Directing angry voices outward would single out targets for blame and further develop group solidarity. To some extent, we could expect to see aspects of politicization in this process, as the group identifies itself against others in ways having to do with relations of power.

Immediate targets for collective, group-affirming anger included Lennon's killer, Mark Chapman. In him, the group confronted an individual who mirrored some of their own experiences and who professed to identify with Lennon. Chapman was close enough to the group that he became the object of subtle scapegoating. As Kai Erikson observes (1966, 22), the need to scapegoat is intensified by the extent to which perpetrators and their victims share the same cultural vocabulary and cultural symbols.

First, I consider Mark Chapman as a conventional news story and look at how writers made "sense" of him and his act, especially in light of his similarity to the "lone assassins" of the 1960s (Lee Harvey Oswald, Sirhan Sirhan, and James Earl Ray). Then I look at ways Mark Chapman was positioned as a scapegoat, at how writers tried set him apart from the sixties generation's ideals and turn him into an outsider. Finally, I consider writings that direct anger outward toward gun control laws and society in general, especially a vision of society in the amorphous impending "Reagan Era."

MAKING SENSE OF MARK CHAPMAN

Though people were shocked by Lennon's sudden, violent death, the sixties generation had experienced the feeling before. Pete Hamill describes it thusly:

> The news arrived like a fragment of some forgotten ritual. . . . If you were there for the sixties, the ritual was part of your life. You went through it for John F. Kennedy and for Martin Luther King, for Malcom X and for Robert Kennedy. The earth shook, and then grief was slowly handled by plunging into newspapers and television shows. (1980, 38)

And like the assassinations of the Kennedys and Martin Luther King, this one lacked a clear and dramatic political or ideological motivation.[1] Mark Chapman surrendered quietly at the scene and offered no explanation for his act for at least one day. The story intitially was what observers, (Gozzi 1989, 35; see also Carey 1987), called a "Crazy World Story"—one that involvles crime and/or violence, features bizarre and unexplained actions seemingly out of character, and offers no clues or suggestions concerning motivations. However, as lawyers for Chapman entered an insanity plea and as information about Chapman emerged, writers grappled with meaning and motivation in various ways. Major stories on Chapman in the *New York Times*, the *Washington Post*, the *Los Angeles Times*, *Newsweek*, *Time*, and *New York* magazine sought meaning in the emerging details of Chapman's life, in speculation on the nature of his mental condition, and in interviews with former friends and acquaintances.

Allan Mayer in *Newsweek*, Pete Hamill in *New York* magazine, John Goldman and Ellen Hume in the *Los Angeles Times*, John Hurst in the *Los Angeles Times*, and Paul Montgomery in the *New York Times* provided substantial biographical sketches in their writings on Chapman. A highly condensed composite of those sketches might read as follows.

Mark Chapman grew up in the suburbs of Atlanta, Georgia. As a teenager in the late 1960s and 1970s he loved the Beatles, especially John Lennon. He also used various drugs including LSD. He then became a so-called "Jesus freak" and criticized Lennon for his antireligious viewpoints. He worked, successfully by all accounts, as a counselor at a local YMCA camp and at a special YMCA camp for

Vietnamese refugees in Arkansas. He was good with children. After the refugee camp closed, Chapman seemed depressed. He enrolled in college but soon dropped out. His girlfriend broke up with him. He moved to Hawaii and attempted suicide. After psychiatric treatment, he began working as a security guard and married a Japanese-American woman older than he. In late 1980 he quit his job and signed the name "John Lennon" in the logbook. He bought a handgun and left for New York. On the afternoon of December 8, 1980, he obtained John Lennon's autograph outside Lennon's residence at the famed Dakota apartments. At about eleven o'clock that night, he stepped from the shadows in the Dakota entranceway and fired five shots from a .38 caliber handgun. Four of the bullets struck Lennon. Chapman quietly surrendered to police at the scene.

In the wake of Chapman's insanity plea and the seemingly "crazy" nature of Chapman's act, Gerald Clarke, in *Time* (1980, 29) and Tom Mathews in *Newsweek* (1980, 34–35), wrote sidebar pieces focusing on Chapman's mental state by emphasizing biographical details that seemed to unfold a story of instability and schizophrenia. The stories, titled "Lethal Delusion" and "Lennon's Alter Ego," respectively, focus on Chapman's intense identification with John Lennon. Clarke wrote:

> To be sure, the parallels that Chapman established between his own life and Lennon's were startling: both loved music as adolescents, both were in rock groups, both loved children, both were devoted to helping others, and both married Asian women who were older than themselves.

Mathews, in *Newsweek,* presents details of Chapman's last three years as a "disintegration" of his personality and suggests that signs of it went largely unnoticed by those close to him. He focuses also on words and acts that seemed to suggest violent tendencies that lurked beneath Chapman's obsessiveness and instability. He concludes by quoting an acquaintance who said, "He was an incredibly hostile individual" (35).

Art Harris, of the *Washington Post* (1980, 6E and 7E) was one of many reporters who found an articulate old friend of Chapman's, rock guitarist Gary Limuti, who was playing in a club band in Atlanta at the time of the killing. Limuti recalled how he and Chapman had idolized Lennon as teenagers and that Chapman was a frustrated musician and an outcast in some ways. Limuti said that, in his mind, Chapman probably wanted to become Lennon and noted similarities in some aspects of their lives. Limuti noted also that Chapman went through a hippie phase after hippies had faded from the cultural scene.

Writings on Chapman tended to reflect an a priori assumption of his insanity. Writing about Chapman's life, then, tended to become an exercise in reporting and arranging details so as to present a picture of an unstable, enigmatic individual. Six months after the killing and just before Chapman was to go to trial, Craig Unger published a long, psychobiography of Chapman in *New York* magazine (1981, 30–32).

Unger allows that Chapman's motivations remain perplexing, but he does link Chapman with John Hinckley, who shot and wounded President Reagan in March 1981. Hinckley professed to be motivated by his love for a mass media figure, young movie actress Jodie Foster. Chapman and Hinckley, according to Unger, shared certain traits: histories of failure, wide personality swings, and weak senses of identity. They both tended to internalize their experiences and became obsessive. Chapman focused on John Lennon, the iconography of Norman Rockwell, and the image of the catcher in the rye from Salinger's novel of that name.

Unger traces Chapman's childhood, which he shows to be less than ideal but also reflective of the times in which he grew up: "Drugs, family strife, broken-hearted love affairs, and rock 'n' roll—Mark grew up carrying more than his share of the banal emotional baggage of suburban adolescence" (31). Those who knew Chapman, Unger reports, say he was suggestible and impressionable. "Mark would occasionally seem to cross the line between exuberance and excess" (31). In addition to Lennon, Chapman worshiped pop musician Todd Rundgren. He often ended letters to friends with quotes from favorite musicians, including Bob Dylan and John Lennon.

As Unger reconstructs Chapman's life, it appears that Chapman's six months of working at the Arkansas YMCA camp was probably the high point of his life. He loved the refugee children and felt he belonged among the staff. He also had a girlfriend he pursued, like his other passions, "without any restraints" (33). The camp at Fort Chaffee closed in December 1975, and Unger writes: "The breakdown had come quickly. From the moment Mark left Fort Chaffee in 1975 virtually everything began to go wrong for him. School, Jessica, the YMCA, his family—one by one the sources from which Mark drew his identity collapsed" (34).

Chapman moved to Hawaii in 1977 and soon attempted suicide. Unger depicts the three years leading up to Lennon's killing as a plunge into obsession and delusion. In attempting to answer why Chapman chose to fixate on Lennon, Unger surmises how Chapman may have linked up Lennon and the scene of the catcher in the rye. Chapman probably saw himself as a savior of the innocent and "like Holden

Caulfield in the novel, Mark would wage his own private war against phoniness" (41). Having failed in his real-life relations, he took refuge in various cultural icons such as Norman Rockwell and John Lennon. But Unger surmises that Chapman "began to perceive Lennon as a hypocrite himself, one who had allowed wealth and success to tarnish the principles he held holy. Mark David Chapman, the catcher in the rye, would go to New York" (35).

Unger's account includes one element of pathos for Chapman. During Chapman's complicated travels after he left Hawaii, ostensibly on his way to New York to kill Lennon, Chapman stopped by the YMCA branch in Atlanta where he had worked with children six years earlier. He had sometimes taken the children out on watermelon hunts, telling them they were looking for dinosaur eggs. The children called him Captain Nemo, after the captain in *20,000 Leagues Under the Sea.* Unger describes Chapman's return thusly:

> Finally, Mark went by the South DeKalb branch of the YMCA. His old boss, Tony Adams, had long since moved on. None of the old staff was there. So he spoke with Pat DeCouq, a swimming instructor who was a relative newcomer. Mark went over to the swimming pool and pointed out a tile with his father's name on it. He asked if anyone still remembered Nemo. No one did. (35)

Unger concludes his piece with a reference to words John Hinckley spoke into a tape recorder a few weeks after Chapman killed Lennon. Hinckley said that Lennon was dead, the world was over, and that anything he might do in 1981 would be solely for Jodie Foster's sake. Unger, like many writers on the subject, keeps close to the subject of Chapman's pathological identification with Lennon, and he draws attention to a similar pathology in John Hinckley.

Some writers on Chapman made ironic references to titles of or lines from Lennon's or Lennon's and McCartney's songs. Craig Unger's piece is titled, "John Lennon's Killer: The Nowhere Man," referring to Lennon's song "Nowhere Man." Pete Hamill titles his section on Chapman in the *New York* magazine piece, "The Long and Winding Road," a bitterly ironic reference to the title of Lennon and McCartney's plaintive love song. Tom Mathews, in *Newsweek*, prefaces his piece by quoting the refrain from Lennon and McCartney's hugely popular "Eleanor Rigby"—"All the lonely people, where do they all come from?" They go on to describe Chapman as "a loner in flight from the barren world of Eleanor Rigby." Other writers made grimly ironic references to Mark Chapman's purchase of the gun he used in the killing. Pete Hamill, in *New York* magazine, notes that the gun shop in Honolulu, where Chapman bought the handgun, prominently displayed this slogan: "Buy a gun and get a bang out of life" (44). Gerald Clarke, in *Time*, quotes the salesman who sold Chapman the gun as saying, "It's the type used by detectives and plainclothes police because it's easy to conceal."

Bill Prochnau organized his *Washington Post* (1980) piece on Chapman around foreshadowing. Prochnau notes various odd acts leading up to the murder and after stating each one uses the refrain, "No one thought much of it" (18A). Craig Unger reported that, as he was leaving Hawaii for New York, Chapman responded to a query from his employment counselor about whether he was looking for another job with the words, "I already have a job to do" (30). Unger also quotes a counselor who worked with Chapman at Fort Chaffee. She remembered that as they all were preparing to leave and saying goodbye Chapman said, "One day one of us is going to be somebody. About five years from now, one of us will do something famous, and it will bring us all together" (33). Unger adds that the words were spoken in December 1975. Several writers (Goldman and Hume, Mayer, Montgomery, and Unger) quoted a Lennon fan who stood with Chapman outside Lennon's residence on the afternoon of the killing. After Chapman had obtained Lennon's autograph, he told someone near him to stay and wait for Lennon to come back out of the Dakota because, "You never know if you'll see him again" (Goldman and Hume, I: 1).

Despite all of the hindsight and reconstructing, most journalists probably would have agreed with Pete Hamill that "the facts don't tell us what was in his [Chapman's] mind . . . nobody knows for sure" (45). However, many writers speaking to the sixties generation judged Chapman in subtle ways, for his history and his obssessive connection to Lennon also connected him uncomfortably with their audience.

MARK CHAPMAN AS SCAPEGOAT

John Lennon was killed by a stranger we had come to know only too well in the 1960s—the lone assassin, who "lacking a sense of who he is, shops among artifacts of our culture, books, movies, TV programs, song lyrics, newspaper clippings—to fashion a character" (McMillan 1982, 16). Mark Chapman's road to the doorway of the Dakota apartments began perhaps during his early teen years around 1970 when a friend described him as "picking over the dying memories of the Beatles generation, searching out hidden meanings in the ashes" (Harris 1980, 6). Chapman, as had Charles Manson a decade earlier, posed special problems for the sixties generation because those bits and pieces of culture out of which he attempted to create himself were often the same symbols, metaphors, and practices that defined and united them. As Turner notes, in liminality, symbols and metaphors may become "dangerously ambiguous" (1974, 273). Chapman, like Manson, appeared to have constructed a twisted tale out of the sixties, and as might be expected in this part of the redressive phase of social drama, the discourse on Chapman took on some elements of scapegoating. As Lennon's death impelled a coming together in the spirit of the old communitas, Chapman was set up against the sixties generation's ideal of themselves. Chapman was marginalized not only for his deed but also for his pathetic "misreading" of the symbols and practices of the sixties.

Writers marginalized Chapman, both explicity and implicitly, in two specific ways. First, Chapman was shown to be both a loner and a follower; having no sense of himself and belonging to nothing, he was set against the ideal of sixties communitas, which simultaneously valorized the individual and the group in its fundamental belief that communal relations were strengthened by individual self-expression (Tipton 1982, 18). Second, the fleeting references to Chapman's bad LSD experiences relegated him to the region of the spiritually damned and set him outside the more limited segmental communitas of shared psychedelic experience.

In newspaper and magazine features, Chapman was described variously as "a college dropout" (Jones 1981, 7), "a 25-year-old former mental patient" (Montgomery 1980, 3), "a former Jesus freak, amateur rock musician, mental patient, and unemployed security guard" (Sager and Wadler 1980, 2A), "a pudgy young man" (Prochnau 1980, 18A), "a suety little man, with a small nose, porky jowls" (Hamill 1980, 42), "an anonymous nobody" (Marcus 1981, 26), and "a 25-year-old doppelganger" and "a loner in flight from the barren world of Eleanor Rigby" (Mayer 1980, 32 and 34). Interestingly, this seemingly piggish, yet ghostly, creature is marginalized by what appear to be both conventional and sixties generation standards. Just as Chapman had pieced together a self out many of the cultural materials of the sixties, so the "puzzling patchwork" of his life (Harris 1980, 6E) came uncomfortably close to mirroring the varied and crooked life paths of many of the sixties generation, but Chapman was pictured as differing from the sixties people in important ways.

He was, for example, "highly suggestible, highly impressionable, intensely eager to prove his worth, [he] was drawn to authority figures as mentors and role models, aping their values" (Unger 1981,

31). A nobody, a virtual ghost, he was portrayed as "rootless, on the move, always searching for that one perfect place" (Hamill 1980, 43). Chapman was set apart by his aloneness, his lack of identity, and, of course, by his pathetic and deadly merging of identities with Lennon. Chapman was shown to be truly a nowhere man, not an individual and not a member of a group.

This scapegoating of Chapman may well have served to further cement feelings of communitas among the grieving sixties generation. Sixties communitas was forged out of a peculiar melding of concepts of the group and the individual. The counterculture universe was monistic—all is one, all is pure energy with no Cartesian self, no subject–object distinction (Tipton 1982, 14–15). In John Lennon's words, "I am he as you are he as you are me as we are all together." The primary object was to be in touch with one's spiritual essence. And the road to group identification lay through the self, for to be in touch with the "all in one" was to be in touch with everyone else also in touch with the same essential reality. As Turner (1974) emphasizes, these individual experiences become the basis for communitas because they are shared. The individual and group blend yet remain distinct. Communitas does not merge identities; rather, identities are released from adherence to social norms and then share an emotional sense of communion via symbols and practices.

Chapman, the nowhere man, obviously had no place in this communitas, which was based in an ideal of strong personal identity *and* shared experience based on the deepening and exploring of that identity. To find the core of the self in sixties communitas was to find the group there also. Chapman was seen as clearly set apart from these conditions, and while nothing about Chapman really could explain his act, he could be constructed in a way so as to set him apart from the mourners, which in turn allowed the group to see itself as having been attacked by an outsider. Chapman was isolated as a deviant, but "the deviant and his more conventional counterpart live in much the same world of symbol and meaning, sharing a similar set of interests in the universe around them . . . [they] are creatures of the same culture, inventions of the same imagination" (Erikson 1966, 20–21). Mark Chapman constructed a twisted tale out of the sixties, and he was reviled all the more for his polluting of the sacred symbols.

Chapman was set apart also by virtue of his inability to accommodate one of the central sacraments of sixties communitas, the LSD experience. Though nothing was said about this explicitly, the mentioning of Chapman's bad experiences on LSD (see for example, Mathews 1980, 34; Unger 1981, 32) suggested another mode of marginalization: that Chapman was unworthy of the sacrament. This example of what I call "counterculture Calvinism" carried over from the problem in the sixties of extolling LSD as a gift from God (for example, Gitlin 1987, 208–9; Leary [1968] 1987, 328–38; Stevens 1988, xiv; Whitmer 1987, 13–37) and rationalizing its occasionally dire effects, from bad trips to full-blown psychosis, a moral predicament that forced many of the sixties generation unwittingly into a conservative posture.

Though steeped in the language and symbolic trappings of Eastern thought and religion, LSD use increasingly became defended on essentially Darwinian and Calvinist grounds. Those who could use LSD were the fit, the elect; those who could not were the weak and the damned—"a cruel kind of natural selection" (Gottlieb 1987, 167). Eastern concepts of reincarnation, caste, and karma also bolstered this view that people are at different levels spiritually; that those who do not achieve certain states of spiritual awareness, in effect, flunk this course called life and must keep taking it over until they get it right. Communitas must be based in some concept of value and worth, so even though sixties communitas was characterized by willful economic and social marginalization, it was based also in a deeply shared sense of spiritual and moral superiority. Whether or not Chapman has "failed" life, much of what was written about him suggests certainly that he failed a tough course in cultural symbolism known as "the sixties."

A contributing factor to this failure may have been Chapman's demographic status as a late baby boomer. Landon Jones, author of a book on the baby boom generation, *Great Expectations* (1980), put a demographic twist on the deeds of Chapman and Ronald Reagan's would-be assassin, John Hinckley. Both were born near the peak of the baby boom in 1955, along with 4,128,000 other Americans. They are right on the cusp dividing old and young baby boomers. Chapman may have shared with many others his age a sense of being locked out of society because of the teeming numbers around him (Jones 1981, 7). He and Hinckley may stand as tragic symbols of a dispossessed demographic cohort that society simply could not accommodate, especially in the ravaged economy of the early 1980s. Figuratively, Chapman is a younger sibling of the older boomers who made up the sixties generation. Just as John Lennon was declaring the dream of the sixties over in 1970, Chapman was sifting through the almost instant ashes of the sixties "scene" looking for meanings.

Much of the writing on Chapman implied that he did not get the right meanings. This particular positioning of Chapman also suggests that Chapman and other late boomers engaged in excorporation: "the process by which the subordinate make their own culture out of the resources and commodities provided by the dominant system" (Fiske 1989, 15; see also, Grossberg 1983–84). In a complex web of segmentation, Chapman and other late boomers may be seen as having fallen under the cultural domination of the older boomers of the sixties generation. The sixties' symbols of an older, educated segment did not automatically transfer to fifteen- and sixteen-year-old kids, who assigned new meanings or simply disregarded the "preferred meanings" of the dominant group. In the case of Mark Chapman, the sixties generation confronts its own status as a cultural establishment. It confronts also the disturbing possibility that the supposed deep, absolute truths of its values and ethos may not be absolute after all. Truth, as the phrase goes, is self-evident. A final irony, disturbing to the sixties generation, is that for all his supposedly twisted excorporation of sixties' symbols, Chapman may have acted symbolically in accordance with certain sixties' values.

Chapman's professed motive for killing Lennon was to save him, as the catcher in the rye saved the children from falling out of innocence, and indirectly to save the sixties that Chapman himself never could experience, never could belong to. Operating, in the end, in a world of pure symbol, image, and dream and from a single-minded desire to preserve innocence and youth, Chapman acted very much in the romantic spirit of sixties communitas. Tragically and ironically he succeeded, as Daniel Stashower suggests in a 1983 article in *American Scholar*:

> Gone now is the John Lennon who once smeared excrement on the walls of his dressing room; who claimed that the Beatles were a bigger item than Christ; and who appeared in a Los Angeles nightclub with a Kotex on his head. In his place is a sort of rock-and-roll Gandhi. Because of his violent death, anything about him that is base or even unkind has been erased. . . . and all because Mark Chapman, standing outside the Dakota apartments, caught him in the rye. (377)

As Charles Manson had a decade earlier, Chapman confounded the counterculture by committing unspeakable acts in its name. Chapman appeared to Lennon literally out of the dark. Symbolically, he fired his gun from that dark side of communitas that could not be contained so easily in the modern mass-mediated, mass cultural contexts of the liminoid, which lacked both ritual and social structures required to contain it. That "the last nail in the coffin of the sixties" could have been set by one of their own was perhaps too terrible for many of the group to contemplate.[2]

GUN CONTROL

John Lennon was the seven-hundred-and-first person shot with a handgun in New York City in 1980 (Bresler 1989, 10). Many nationally known journalists located in the New York–Washington, D.C.–Los Angeles axis reacted to Lennon's death with pieces on gun control. Lennon's murder came soon after the murder of Dr. Michael Halberstam, a noted doctor, writer, and televison commentator in Washington, D.C. Halberstam surprised a burglar in his home and was shot to death with a handgun. The two cases often were linked in the ensuing intensification of the ongoing national debate over crime and handgun control. Just two weeks before his death, Halberstam had spoken out for handgun control in a commentary broadcast on the Cable News Network (see Shields 1980).

A substantial amount of pro–gun-control writing expressed frustration with continued political inaction due to the power of the National Rifle Association. In a *Los Angeles Times* op-ed piece, Nelson T. Shields, chairman of Handgun Control, Inc., expressed hope that the nation's youth would respond to Lennon's death by mounting a gun-control campaign against the National Rifle Association (NRA) similar to the sixties antiwar movement (1980, IV: 5). But Haynes Johnson, in the *Washington Post*, argued that calls for gun control in the wake of the deaths of Lennon and Halberstam would "add nothing new to the debate." Marshaling a pile of statistics on handgun murders, Johnson argued that common sense dictated some kind of gun control policy, but he also admitted to seeing "no prospects for change" due to the strength of the gun lobby, lamenting that "for more than 40 years since George Gallup took his first poll on American attitudes about gun control legislation, the public overwhelmingly has endorsed such things as the licensing of handguns. And nothing has happened" (1980, A3). Another *Washington Post* writer, Colman McCarthy, described the NRA as a "wealthy, well-staffed and blustery lobby . . . [which] has weathered so many of these storms in the past few years— Robert Kennedy, George Wallace, Allard Lowenstein, Sen. John Stennis, George Moscone, to name only politicians—that it can sail on with its eyes closed. . . . The NRA wins another shootout. Nothing changes" (1980, A23). A letter to the *Washingon Post* attributed the NRA's position purely to profit motive rather than to philosophical arguments about freedom (Tepper 1980, A20).

Mark Chapman shot John Lennon with a Charter Arms .38 caliber pistol, the same type of gun Arthur Bremer used to shoot George

Wallace in 1972. Mike Royko, in his nationally syndicated column, was moved to angry satire, noting that Charter had demanded an apology from CBS News back in 1972 when its report described Bremer's weapon as a cheap handgun. Royko noted he was "pleased to see the stories reporting the death of John Lennon were specific and accurate about the kind of gun used to murder the world-renowned musician." Royko deadpanned that it was important to "show proper respect for an excellent gun such as the Charter .38" (1980, *Los Angeles Times*, II: 11).

President-elect Ronald Reagan, who three months later would be wounded by a handgun in an assassination attempt, rejected gun control as an appropriate response to Lennon's murder and suggested instead tougher federal sentences for the use of a handgun in the commission of a crime (the *New York Times*, 1980, December 10, I: 34). *Rolling Stone's* Dave Marsh, in response, accused Reagan of senility and charged "It is still infuriating that in the present political environment we'll probably never get the chance to find out what effect such laws might have" (1981, 28).

Tom Wicker, in the *New York Times*, placed blame on the public. Arguing that gun control was a rational and solid proposition and charging the gun lobby with "sophistry and self-delusion," he nevertheless despaired that nothing would be done and that more lives would be lost needlessly simply because the society was not yet ready for gun control. We irrationally believe guns will protect us, he argued, and "the truth is that that perverted demand from you and me is so great that politicians cannot stand against it" (1980, I: 35).

While gun-control forces argued that Americans had an irrational, emotional attachment to guns, gun-freedom writers countered with their own accusations of emotionalism. H. L. Richardson charged in the *Los Angeles Times* that gun-control arguments in the wake of Lennon's and Halberstam's deaths were emotional and focused only on the weapon instead of the criminal. The issue is that of controlling crime, not guns (1980, IV: 5). Anti–gun-control arguments also focused on perceived contradictions in "liberal" thought: "With one hand, liberals will use the Lennon case to promote gun confiscation, and with the other they will cheerfully free Lennon's murderer if the arresting police forget so little as to dot an 'I'" (Anderson 1980, I: 18). Similarly, Stanton Evans (1981, 7) wrote in *Human Events*, "Of course, it is precisely the people who inveigh against tough punishment of criminals who are most fervent in their demands for gun control. . . . Those who refuse to punish the guilty invariably foist the consequences of that refusal on the innocent." Evans implicitly indicted liberal impulses of the 1960s, claiming that various social and legal reforms from that period, such as "massive programs of social uplift, rehabilitationist penology, release of violent criminals back into society [and] de facto abolition of capital punishment [reflected] the belief that people aren't responsible for committing crimes and other anti-social acts" (7).

Members of the sixties generation directed anger at guns and the gun lobby, and their voices simply joined the larger chorus of this aspect of the social drama begun in the 1960s that divided Americans along urban/rural and middle-class/working-class lines. Certainly, in the national discourse on gun control, the sixties generation took a back seat to older liberals who incorporated Lennon into their existing arguments. And the sixties generation had to confront the realities of power relations in American society; they and the older liberals were no match for the powerful National Rifle Association. Turner suggests (1985, 220) that in the resolution of a social drama, "there can never be a complete replication of the social state before the social drama declared itself. Former allies may have become opponents. New allegiances will have been made." Sixties people who drew political battle lines over gun control in response to Lennon's death also found themselves amid new alliances with older liberals whom they had scorned in the sixties and even with some police groups who had turned against the NRA when it advocated the unrestricted sale of so-called "cop killer" plastic-nosed bullets that could easily pierce the Kevlar vests worn by police.

SOCIETY AND THE REAGAN ERA

Had Lennon been assassinated in 1970, there would have been little problem in targeting President Richard Nixon as a recipient of anger and as a symbol of all that contradicted Lennon and the sixties generation. Reagan himself had been an object of segmental scorn as governor of California during the height of the hippie and student radical movements. Some writers viewed his impending inauguration as an ominous sign that could only bolster the notion of the death of the sixties. *Rolling Stone* writers Dave Marsh and Greil Marcus grappled with the notion of the culpability of the Reagan Era, but neither could advance a coherent argument to connect it solidly with Lennon's murder.

Dave Marsh, in a piece titled "Ghoulish Beatlemania," (1981), reads into Reagan's response to Lennon's death a callousness that goes beyond the issue of gun control, arguing that to equate Lennon's death with street crime is to say it was random. But Marsh recites a list that includes the Kennedys, Martin Luther King, the 1979 Jonestown mass suicide and murder in Guyana, Allard Lowenstein, Harvey Milk, and George Moscone. If Lennon's death is placed in this context, says Marsh, it shows that the message of the past two years is clear: "Human life has never been cheaper . . . what we're mourning now is the end of a time when all of us held human life dear" (29). Asking us to accept that life is cheaper in the United States in 1980 than it was in ancient Rome, Nazi Germany, or Stalinist Russia, Marsh also offers his list of victims with no explanation of the connections. Possibly Marsh perceives a very close relationship with his *Rolling Stone* audience, which allows him to make such a list and believe in its liturgical effect to convey meaning, resorting to nonlinear, associational cognitive modes valued by the sixties generation (see Tipton 1982).

The message seems to be that we have entered a dark and violent time marked by the rejection of values (the dearness of human life) espoused by Lennon and the sixties generation. Marsh appeals to old emotions and old stereotypes and relies on simple juxtaposition to bypass logic. Just how a mass suicide/murder in a small religious cult and a disgruntled employee shooting his superiors herald a new era remains unexplained. Nor does Marsh connect these events clearly to Lennon's murder. The "us versus them" division is murky. Who are "we," other than an ethereal collection who "held life dear"? And who are the never-named "they"?

Greil Marcus, in his essay "Life and Life Only" (1981), proposes that Lennon's killing represented a "radical change in the nature of public discourse in the United States over the past year" (27). In Reagan's election Marcus sees the ascendance of a puritanical religious right wing that divides the world into the saved and the damned:

> It is as if the Puritans have reached across 300 years of American history to reclaim the society they once founded—accepting the worst vulgarizations of their beliefs if it means that, once again, God and his servants will be able to look upon America and tell the elect from the reprobate, the redeemed from the damned. (27)

Marcus echoes the counterculture's rebellion against "biblical authoritarianism" (Tipton, 15), which seemed defeated in the sixties but now rises in the person of Ronald Reagan in 1980. Though this Calvinist creed of the elect and damned did not directly inspire Chapman to kill Lennon, Marcus says such a message suggests that certain people are innocent and others are to blame; thus Chapman's "private madness" is given tacit public justification:

If Klansmen and Nazis had the right to kill communists in Greensboro, and a jury said they did, then on a certain moral level you and I and Mark Chapman have the right to kill whoever it is that troubles our lives. (27)

This new Calvinism threatens the ethic of tolerance and pluralism central to the sixties counterculture and is seen as providing justification for acts of repression and violence against "others," if those others are "evil." Though Marcus does not mention it, readers could process his argument in the context of news accounts of Mark Chapman's religious "conversion" that immediately followed his brief period of drug use and identification with John Lennon and the counterculture.

In retrospect it is easy to claim that Marcus did identify a real political enemy for both the sixties generation and older and younger liberals. The new religious right that seemed to them to loom ominously in 1980 has not influenced national politics to the extent Marcus and many others feared, perhaps because members of the sixties generation have joined with other segments in combating the religious right on various political and social fronts, especially the abortion issue. Though Marcus's connection between Lennon's murder and the religious right is tenuous, he appears to have identified an object for anger and subsequent political action for many of the sixties generation. Although the impending Reagan Era could not clearly be linked to Lennon's death, it did subsequently bring with it a sustained conservative attack on the sixties and the sixties generation.

THE UNLIKELIHOOD OF SEPARATION

Separation was an idea rather than an actual possibility. Discourses of nostalgia and anger provided ways for the sixties generation to call itself together to celebrate its shared emotions, values, and antagonisms. Anger was a way of marking its differences from the larger society. In 1980, though, the sixties generation perhaps could call itself together primarily in memory. Its discourse of anger was thin and was easily deflated in larger political and cultural contexts. It did not make "us versus them" distinctions very clearly. The problem of naming objects of anger in 1980 reflects the weakness of a group identity that was formed in the liminoid oppositional spaces of the sixties.

By comparison, consider how writings on Lennon's death might have looked if he had been shot in 1970 instead of 1980. In the waning days of the counterculture in 1970, Lennon's death likely would have sparked immediate accusations of government conspiracies to silence Lennon because of his political views. Beyond that, it might well have been seen as evidence of the violence and decadence of "straight" society. A killer like Chapman (for Chapman himself was only fifteen in 1970) would have been portrayed as a former counterculture ally who went astray, reincorporating with the sick structures of straight society by turning back to religion. His act would have been seen as a vindication of the counterculture's claim that straight society was violent and sick at its core, that its impulse was to kill symbols and voices of freedom and truth which threatened it, just as it waged war on peasants in Southeast Asia and on blacks and students at home. In such a strident, hyperbolic discourse Richard Nixon would have been a perfect embodiment of the enemy.

December 1980 did not even present a convenient symbol of national leadership for attack. The country was, in effect, between leaders. Jimmy Carter was leaving office and Ronald Reagan had yet to assume leadership, a situation that well reflects the confused context of assigning blame and directing anger. Some of this confusion had to do with the generation's half-hearted drifting back into structure and their loss of a clear segmental identity. As Todd Gitlin (1987, 424) observed:

> The youth movement's collapse left not only political wreckage but a spiritual and psychological crisis—and not only for the onetime hard core, but for the larger penumbra of part-time activists and the less-committed young middle class as well. Many verities had collapsed fast in the Sixties, and no vigorous way of life had grown up in their place. Confusion abounded. Traditional authority had lost its hold, but what alternative principles should replace it?

The objects of anger following Lennon's death did not always reflect the exclusive concerns of this segment. Handgun laws, the Reagan Era, and Mark Chapman presented more specifically generational and segmental targets, but the fact that Lennon's death could be appropriated quite easily, for example, by the larger social goal of gun control gives evidence that the sixties generation did not have exclusive control over its heroes and that it had itself moved more into the mainstream.

This discourse of separation reflects, among other things, the instability of identity that characterizes the social disorganization inherent in social drama. Identities formed in the liminoid communitas of the sixties were fleeting. Yet many elegists for Lennon wrote as if 1980 identities were no more secure. Fred Davis has suggested (1979) that nostalgia for the fifties in mainstream American culture in the 1970s reflected an uneasiness with the disorder of the sixties. The strong impulse toward nostalgia for the sixties in writings on Lennon suggests that the sixties generation felt uneasy about the 1970s and prospects for the 1980s. It suggests that many still were unsure of their coordinates of individual identity. The discourse of separation called the group together in ways that suggested an instability of meaning in the present and an impulse to embrace the past.

NOTES

1. As might have been expected, a book advancing a conspiracy theory of Lennon's murder finally did appear. British lawyer and writer Fenton Bresler argues in *Who Killed John Lennon?* (1989) that Mark Chapman was programmed to kill Lennon by the CIA, much in the manner depicted in the 1962 movie *The Manchurian Candidate*. The motive, according to Bresler, was that the CIA feared Lennon would become a rallying point for political protest once the Reagan administration launched its "reactionary programme" (6). The focus of the book is mostly on the "spy-thriller" aspects of the CIA programming of Chapman. It does, however, implicitly attribute great power to Lennon and to what was left in 1980 of the student left and counterculture.

2. In 1992 a book on Mark Chapman appeared. Jack Jones's *Let Me Take You Down* is the result of five years of interviews and correspondence with Chapman. The book is marketed as a crime and psychological study rather than as a social/cultural study. The jacket notes proclaim it "invites comparison with *In Cold Blood* and *Executioner's Song*." Jones's work does flesh out earlier journalistic biographies and profiles done under the heat of deadlines. It also documents Chapman's "bad trips" on LSD. Jones quotes Todd Gitlin who says, "Those who did a lot of drugs without any supervision . . . were often unable to bear up." (107). Chapman also revealed to Jones that the first time he ever felt he belonged was among his drug-taking, hippie friends. Chapman, who had much difficulty in being accepted at school and was often the target of bullies, said this was the first time he ever felt among an "in" group (103). These revelations seem to support my contention in this chapter that Chapman posed problems for the Lennon mourners because he did identify, however briefly and tenuously, with counterculture communitas.

Part Three

Voices of Reintegration

5

Resignation

Social drama, in its full development, changes certain beliefs and agendas, which occur over a wide range of segments, into some form of consensual meaning (Turner 1985, 203), for even separation requires the proverbial "agreement to disagree." Reintegration reflects a search for what Carey calls an enlarged human community and the impulse toward a common culture (1985, 41). The goal of reintegration is served when various redressive acts reflect on the group's history and myths, not just attempt to reproduce them. Redressive rituals for groups often show "an effort to have [their] past make sense in the situation of their particular collective present" (Moore and Meyerhoff, quoted in Turner 1985, 200). One place this type of reflective evaluation of the past occurred for the sixties generation was in the loose ritual form of mass-mediated grieving for John Lennon. While the voices of separation discussed in the previous two chapters tended toward unreflective immersion in the past, the voices of reintegration show efforts to reconstruct memory in terms of the "particular collective present."

To that end, reintegration discourse tended to accept the notion of "the death of the sixties." To accept the death of Lennon as the death of the sixties was essentially a reintegrative move. If the sixties still live then the old divisions live, too, since those divisions define sixties communitas as much as shared experiences and values, but by 1980, both the divisions and the feelings of sharing had blurred and receded for the sixties generation. On the symbolic level, it seemed the feelings called "the sixties" had to die in order for reintegration with the larger social order to occur. Much of what I call active reintegrative discourse on Lennon accepted the death of the sixties as a kind of transformation and often pointed to ways Lennon had led the sixties generation toward change and growth. A much smaller part of the discourse saw the death of the sixties as final. The old values, in this view, were ineffective, the old feelings dead. These writings suggested implicitly that there was nothing left but reintegration. In Lennon's death, the group finally had dissolved, and hope had been lost. These latter voices express a fundamentally depressive outlook on the death of the sixties and a mood of grim resignation about reintegration with the social order.

THE LOST DREAM

"Anyone who doubted that the 1960s are dead ought to be convinced now." So opens a piece titled "John Lennon and the Death of the '60s" (1980) by *Dallas Times Herald* columnist Bryan Woolley.

The picture of Woolley that accompanies the column shows a fortyish man with slightly long hair and a beard. He seems in appearance to be an insider in the generational discourse, but he refers to the sixties generation as "they," not "we." The sixties have died, proposes Woolley, because youthful rebels asked the right questions but came up with the wrong answers.

Woolley writes that a "nice lady" phoned him the day after Lennon's death to say she was sorry about it but that she always thought the Beatles had an evil influence on America's youth. "'Not as evil as Elvis, maybe, but evil.'" She thought the Class of '57 at Highland Park High School was "'the last stable group we've produced.'" Woolley observes, though, that it was just those 1957 values that the young of the sixties challenged. They asked valid questions, he says, about segregation, the role of military force, and materialism. However, the generation's answers such as LSD, communes, and nihilistic political acts "weren't always wonderful." And now in 1980, the ideals expressed in the generation's questioning are being trampled by a reactionary political mood.

Lennon's death is ironic, says Woolley, because it came "when he and most of his generation were trying to get along as quietly and peacefully as possible with a world they couldn't change." The sixties generation "still haven't become accustomed to their ideals lying in ruins and their heroes being gunned down." He concludes, with perhaps a hint of exasperation, "I don't know why that is. They've had plenty of experience of both." The death of the sixties for Woolley is final, and a generation's ideals appear to have been defeated by the vastly more powerful forces of a world they could not change.

Boston Globe staffer Christina Robb suggests in her piece "We need

him . . . we miss him" (1980) that the values of the sixties generation
are ineffective, though not necessarily wrong or misguided. Robb alludes to the Beatles' 1968 animated fantasy film, *Yellow Submarine*,
which she had seen again just a few weeks before Lennon's death.
The villains of the story are called the blue meanies. They look much
like turn-of-the-century English policemen and can turn their hands
into guns. In the wake of Lennon's death, Robb says, "We know too
much about the blue meanies now. We know they have guns, and if
you fight guns with love, you end up with guns."

The blue meanies were, at the time of *Yellow Submarine* (and remain for Robb) a metaphor for an unenlightened, generic violence that
the sixties generation believed lay at the core of modern America. Its
members thought they could overcome that violence with love; that is
what happens in *Yellow Submarine*. Writing in a childlike tone and
from a child's perspective, Robb says, "The grownups will just have
to take the guns away." However, she quotes Lennon, "There aren't
any grownups. Just human bein's [*sic*]." The possibililty that there
really are no grownups suggests problems that many sixties people had
with reintegration, the feeling that the larger society was unstable, that
order and form were not always apparent in it. She asks:

> Then who's going to take the guns away. I mean if there aren't any
> grownups then the children with guns will just go on getting bigger
> and bigger guns, won't they? And you know it spreads. The bigger guns
> get, the more of us they belong to. (19)

A world threatened by nuclear war is a world, Robb suggests, without
grownups and without love or reason. It seems in 1980 to be no different from the world the sixties generation rebelled against.

As Robb portrays a legacy of ineffective ideals in a world without
guidance and moral leadership, an editorial in the same issue of the
Boston Globe (The Lennon connection, 1980) calls all values and
meanings into question. It remarks that the generation that grew up
with Lennon was finding it "sad and scary to realize that survival has
less to do with how one chooses to live one's life . . . than with the
cruelties of chance, the accidents of fate." That lesson in Lennon's
death seems "an inauspicious prologue for the decade still to come."

THE UTOPIAN VISION BETRAYED

Pieces by Greil Marcus and Ken Kesey in *Rolling Stone* and by
Robert Christgau in the *Village Voice* argue that John Lennon held

together a utopian image for the sixties generation and that he was killed because he offered hope. Hope now seems defeated.

Marcus, in "Life and Life Only" (1981), says the Beatles offered a romantic image of utopia "that could encompass every desire for love, for family, for friendship. . . . It shaped one's sense of possibility and loss, of the worth of things"(26). That utopia was grounded, though, by John Lennon "in wit, contingency, doubt and struggle" (26). Lennon was the reality principle of the Beatles, and that, says Marcus, is why so many became obsessed with him. In the 1970s, in Marcus's words the time of "post-Beatle culture," it was Lennon who "more than anyone else . . . communicated the truth that some image of utopia was necessary" (26). Lennon's vision, Marcus asserts, was not solipsistic. It assumed the existence of and connection with other people. Marcus implies that what was left of sixties communitas survived in Lennon's music and in ways that music and the feelings about Lennon connected members of the sixties generation.

Marcus accepts that this vision may have died with Lennon, but in his death that deep connectedness was felt, painfully, once more. He says he felt "overwhelming despair" in seeing other people's reactions to Lennon—a black armband on a white-shirted office worker, a picture of Lennon on a store counter: "Those were the things that did it, that made the last sixteen years collapse on my head as if now it was time to pay for every moment of pleasure, affection and friendship they had contained" (27). In his conclusion, Marcus suggests the ephemeral nature of sixties communitas as a mass-mediated phenomenon. Four days after Lennon was shot, Marcus says he woke up to find Beatles music off the radio and the story off the front page: "I scanned the front page again to see if I'd missed anything: I ran the radio dial across the stations. Nothing. Does this mean, I thought, that it's over: That he's not dead anymore?" (27).

Robert Christgau, in the *Village Voice* (1980, 1), seems to attribute Lennon's death to the perils of fame in the contemporary world but concludes that Lennon was killed because he was a leader as well as a celebrity; in addition to mere pleasure, he offered hope. Christgau opens his piece by recounting a meeting with Lennon and Ono in 1971. Saying he was never one to hobnob with stars, Christgau tells his *Village Voice* audience that Lennon "had always been my own personal Beatle and probably yours." Lennon was the Beatle "we" might have known—the artist, the intellectual, the bohemian.

Christgau relates a comment Lennon made about fame back in 1971 in a hotel suite. Ringo Starr complained that he had called room service an hour earlier and no food had arrived. Lennon asked Starr if he'd told them who he was. Ringo said no. "Well, why not?" Lennon asked, "You've got the fucking fame—you might as well get something out of it." At once cynical, Lennon's remark was also an ironic comment on the nature of his, and the Beatles', fame. Christgau says that Lennon, more than most pop stars, "tried to do good with his fame, but that doesn't mean he had much success." He chronicles Lennon's well-known failures in that vein (the "bed-in" for peace, for example) but praises his last album, *Double Fantasy*, for its candor. It made Christgau believe than Lennon might make good rock and roll when he was sixty. But now, Christgau quotes Lennon, "The dream is over."

Lennon seems to have been killed as a result of his fame. Christgau wonders about Mark Chapman but believes, whatever his stated motives, "the underlying pathology would be the same—the anonymous eating the famous like a cannibal feeding on testicles." But that explanation, he says, is too simple. Lennon's fame was special because he held out hope: "He never lost that utopian identification." But to hold out hope is to risk disappointing people, because Lennon's "power" was really quite limited. It was good for room service, as Lennon said, and it could not solve anyone else's problems. Disappointment will turn to resentment and hate for supposedly true believers like Chapman. But the hope and utopian dreams have not come to pass for anyone else either, implies Christgau.

Ken Kesey closes his *Rolling Stone* piece, "On the Passing of John Lennon," (1981), with much the same thought. He re-creates a conversation with writer Hunter Thompson, another famous counterculture figure. Thompson wonders why assassins target people like John Lennon and not him: "I mean, I've pissed off a lot of people in my time" (68). Kesey replies, "But you never disappointed them. You never promised World Peace or Universal Love" (68).

In the Marcus, Christgau, and Kesey pieces, the "hope" that Lennon held out and that now has died has to do with Lennon as articulator of sixties communitas. Lennon was a powerful artist, but he could not have moved beyond mere entertainment to become a symbol of hope and utopia without an audience willing to make him that symbol. That is to say, Lennon, with a certain degree of awareness, came to articulate existing feelings born in a generation's liminoid experiences in the sixties. Marcus, Christgau, and Kesey all attribute cultural power to Lennon, and these pieces mourn the end of powerful collective feelings of hope that coalesced around him.

FROM SIXTIES DREAMS TO EIGHTIES NIGHTMARES

I conclude this section by returning to Ken Kesey's elegy for Lennon in *Rolling Stone* (1981). The third in his trinity of visitations was from "the ghost, I fear, of Christmases to come: Patrick the Punk" (68). Kesey's attempt to deal with Patrick foregrounds the problem of the suitability of counterculture ideals in the world of 1980. Earlier in the piece, Kesey revives feelings of communitas centered on shared memories in his encounter with John the Groupie, but Patrick the Punk seems an embodiment of the present.

He was walking up the road to the Kesey place; Kesey picked him up. Only "a few years past voting age," his face was half covered with white lotion to combat a case of poison ivy. Sullen, he rambled on about "fucking, blood sucking vampires." Broke, he wanted Kesey to get him on with a country and western band: "He stank of medicine and nicotine and sour unvented adrenalin of rage—and I didn't want to let him stroll onto my place" (68). Kesey lets him "ramble on about all the fucking revolutionary sellouts and nut-cutting feminist harpies and brain-crippling shrinks and mother-raping bulls who run this dark fucking world" (68).

Kesey's reaction to Patrick is both shamanistic and psychotherapeutic, reflecting what Steven Tipton has observed as the mixed meanings that make up the world of the counterculture individual and the mixed moral logic that governs action in it (1982, 14). Kesey equates the darkness he perceives in Patrick's soul with the darkness of the impending winter solstice and says he knows the kid "came as a kind of barometer, a revelation of the nation's vibrational climate" (68). He tells Patrick that things will get better again, basing his prophecy on the simple act of faith that light will follow the dark. But Patrick sneers, "Get better? With seventy percent of the nation voting for a second-rate senile actor who thinks everybody on welfare should be castrated?" (68). Patrick obviously is not buying the old cosmic harmony notion. Kesey reaches for the next arrow in his ethical quiver: "Listen to me punk," he growls. "Don't you know you got to change your mind? That the way you're thinking, tomorrow is gonna be worse than today. . . . Until you're finally going to simply *go out!*" (68). Kesey's words echo those of Lennon in 1980: "You've got to create your own dream." If he and the punk do not share the same feelings that generate the old cosmic community, then Kesey must slip into a more contemporary version of self-management, more est than zen. Patrick is not buying this either. "Mister, I don't give a fuck," he says (68).

Helping Patrick out of the truck, Kesey feels in the punk's duffel bag something "hard and ominous . . . about the size and shape of an Army .45" (68). Although he makes no overt comparison, the narrative implies the connection with Lennon. Kesey, a lesser counterculture celebrity, is stalked by one of "this new legion of the dangerous disappointeds" who wants something from him. Kesey finally seems to get rid of Patrick but worries, "I don't know what to do about him. He's out there and on the rise" (68). As Patrick walks away, Kesey says he feels crosshairs on the back of his neck (68).

Kesey's final parable does much to question and undercut counterculture myth. The essay shows counterculture ethics as helpless in the face of Patrick the Punk. The political message is murky. It is too facile to blame Reaganism for Patrick, and Kesey does not push that argument. It is just as easy to blame the Patricks for Reaganism; in the days of the counterculture, the marginalized, the dropouts, were the heroes; now they are scary. Patrick is young, rebellious, disaffected, as were his sixties compatriots, but he seems totally without ideals, and in Patrick's dark loneliness, Kesey sees nothing so much as the absence of both structure and communitas. The Patricks are out there. They'll take everything. They don't care.

CRISIS OF SPIRIT

Most of the pieces I analyzed in this chapter reflect an overwhelming sense of loss and intense feelings of sorrow. By acknowledging the death of the sixties, they propose reintegration by default, as it were. They do not look to a future; instead they mourn the loss of the past. They do not, as most nostalgia does, celebrate. They propose that communitas is dead with Lennon and resign themselves to reintegration.

This crisis of spirit is connected to material conditions. The potential receptiveness of the sixties generation to depressive evaluations of Lennon's death may also have been associated with their perception of their relative positions in the social order. The sense of spiritual loss may have been magnified by a corresponding sense of material loss. The 1970s were difficult economic times for many Americans, and the entire cohort of baby boomers has lagged behind earlier generations across all economic indicators (Light 1988, 48). Well-educated boomers, who made up much of the counterculture, suffered demographic crowding well into the 1980s. Annie Gottlieb presumes to speak for an increasingly marginalized sixties generation when she says, "In the early Eighties, all we knew was that we were poor and insecure, and our ideals were to blame" (1987, 325).

The voices of resignation articulated a distinct sense of social dislocation among members of the sixties generation. The writings examined in this chapter read into Lennon's death and the preceding decade a virtual destruction of the segment's identity based in the communitas symbolized by Lennon. Those old identities steeped in idealism and a sense of communion are seen as either wrong and foolish to begin with or as too fragile to survive the reality of day-to-day struggles in the context of the larger social order. These voices do not praise the social order; indeed they suggest sometimes that it has crushed their ideals and old identity forms. They suggest a state of cultural homelessness.

6

Acceptance

Voices of acceptance looked toward ways of reintegrating with the social order without having to repudiate the sense of a shared past, and also without obliterating the past, as do some of the voices of resignation. In John Lennon many could find a symbol for reintegration in the way his later private life demonstrated how the sixties generation could move into adulthood at least partly on its own terms. Many writers find in Lennon a possible model for reintegration by focusing on him as a symbol of adjustment to eighties life rather than as a symbol of sixties communitas. The mode of acceptance proposes, also, a more grounded relationship between Lennon and his generation.

The old communitas relationship to Lennon took place in the counterculture context of a timeless, transcendental realm of emotional communion; it had about it an aura of pure and unchanging cosmic truth. It was that timeless place of spiritual communion where Scott Spencer suggests "we" could "be" Lennon and feel what he felt just before his death (1981). It is this state and this mode of relation with Lennon that often is celebrated nostalgically. Voices of acceptance, however, engage not a mystic, static truth; rather, in Yeats's words, they "commend . . . whatever is begotten, born, and dies." They bring Lennon back into time and history. Lennon's death is seen as transformation; and his, and the generation's, life are seen in terms of progress, growth, and change.

In acceptance, Lennon is considered often in his structural roles as husband and father. The family, in counterculture thinking, was often another expression of ecstasy; in the mode of acceptance, it is a source of security and peace. Family also requires obligation. Lennon once explained his devotion to his newborn son quite simply: "It's owed"

(O'Toole 1980, 39). Also, voices of acceptance view generational identity more in the material and historical context of the larger society,
not as a manifestation of emotional communion. These voices for in-
corporation elegize Lennon in three primary ways: (1) They emphasize Lennon's post-Beatles life and his personal and artistic progress
and development. (2) They consider Lennon's and Yoko Ono's relationship, apart from structural roles, as an example of growth, exper-
imentation, and artistic collaboration. In doing this, some also address
the issue of sexism in the counterculture. (3) They explicitly criticize
the use of Lennon as a symbol for communitas.

STRUCTURAL FAMILY

Jay Cocks's *Time* magazine cover story, "The Last Day in the Life"
(1980, 18–24), the longest piece on Lennon that appeared in the major national newspapers and magazines, is organized around the theme
of "family" and is strongly present-oriented. Cocks gently contexts the
sixties as just a part of a longer life journey, shying away from re-
creating or valorizing what Todd Gitlin calls, "the millennial, all-or-
nothing mood of the Sixties" (1987, 437). The elegy begins and ends
with images of family and posits Lennon as a survivor, emphasizing
the terrible irony of having to write about the death of a survivor.
Lennon is shown to be, despite his wealth and fame, one of "us" now,
an example of a generation beginning to make sense of its life and
Lennon's life in more traditional ways.

Cocks opens with a terse re-creation of the shooting, "Just a voice
out of the American night, Mr. Lennon" (18), and moves quickly to
describe the pathos of the grieving wife and son, quoting Yoko Ono's
account of how she tried to explain his father's death to their five-
year-old son, Sean. Cocks quickly and firmly situates the elegy in the
real world of death and grieving. The account of the boy's trouble in
comprehending the sudden death hearkens back to generational memories of the sudden, incomprehensible assassinations of the sixties.

But there is another family, the emotional, generational family, and
its mention suggests conflicted notions of family carried over from
the sixties: "Not just for his wife and son but for more people than
anyone could ever begin to number, the killing of John Lennon was a
death in the family" (18). Lennon's death brings many of the sixties
generation to consider expanded concepts of the family, especially as
they appeared in the counterculture.

It was common in the sixties for various groups of musicians or social action collectives or people who just happened to be in the same place at the same time to call themselves families. The yearning for family could be seen as a reaction to the segmentation and privatization of modern life, but, at the same time, the term "generation gap," spawned in the sixties, suggested a society in which parents and children could not communicate because their basic values appeared to differ so widely. Often rejecting family at the structural level—family as home—the counterculture conceived of family on an intuitive, emotional level. Its "theological monism" (Tipton 1982, 14) posited that to be in touch with the "all in one," or transcendent reality, was to be in deep communion with anyone else in touch with the "all in one." The key here is the counterculture notion of transcendent, mystical reality accessible to all via drugs, music, meditation, or some form of deep experience. In the counterculture, *family*, a word traditionally suggesting deep structural ties of obligation, came to be used casually to describe the relations of those in touch with the same experience or objects. The deeper the shared emotion regarding the same object of contemplation or adoration, the more likely fellow experiencers were to see themselves as family.

Cocks pays brief homage to this collective memory of family composed of "everyone who cherished the sustaining myth of the Beatles—which is to say . . . much of an entire generation that is passing, as Lennon was at age 40, into middle age" (18). But even as he pays homage to the old notion of family, Cocks turns to the present time of middle age. And having celebrated the old concept of group, he turns his attention to the individual, to Lennon's uniqueness.

Cocks argues that what we have lost in Lennon are imagination and genius. Lennon, says Cocks, was a great risk taker who forever changed rock and roll. He is linked with one of America's great poets, as Cocks asserts that Lennon's music "seemed to be torn from that small stormy interior where, as Robert Frost once wrote, 'work is play for mortal stakes'" (20).

Cocks also turns away from generational solipsism, cautioning that both the familial sense of communion and the awe for Lennon's genius are not shared by all. Despite the worldwide interest in Lennon's death, Cocks notes, "Lennon remained chiefly the property—one might even be tempted to say prisoner—of his own generation" (20). There are those who see the Beatles as only a "benign cultural curiousity" and those who see Lennon as just a rich songwriter prone to foolish outbursts; there are many who wonder "what all the fuss is about" (20). The young, especially, seem puzzled and distanced by the mourning. Cocks quotes a Chicago high-schooler who agreed the death was the end of an era—"my mom's," she said (20).

After further biographical review, Cocks returns at the end of his piece to Lennon's structural family, with all its messiness, all its hurts. He takes special notice of Julian, Lennon's teenaged son from his first marriage. Cocks emphasizes that he felt Julian, in the wire-service photographs, looked particularly pained, "haunted" even. Cocks is compelled to confront, gently to be sure, that Lennon had, in effect, abandoned his son when he left Cynthia Lennon to live with and eventually marry Yoko Ono. When Julian was small during the early days of the Beatles, Lennon saw little of him. Cocks reminds us that Lennon was abandoned at age four by his natural mother and raised by an aunt as a consequence of his father deserting the family. Lennon's mother reunited with him but died when he was fourteen. Cocks submits that Julian, like his father, had lost a parent twice. He mentions, too, how Lennon doted over his new son, Sean.

Lennon, Cocks concludes sentimentally, had what everybody wanted (fame and fortune) but "wanted only what so many others have, and take for granted. A home and a family. Some still center of love. A life. One minute more" (24).

Cocks holds the past and the present in equilibrium. He invites readers to see themselves and Lennon both as part of a mystical family suspended in time, in their memories, and to see Lennon as they are today, struggling with the simple things that all are likely to take for granted, especially the demands, the triumphs, and the pains of structural family. Cocks's last words seem simultaneously a paen to the quiet satisfaction of the normal progress of life and an evocation of the feel of the sixties. Those last words speak the catchword of the sixties, "love," and they faintly echo the mystic bent of the sixties in the image of the "still center." Cocks seems to suggest here that Lennon's life may exemplify how we can dissolve the sixties into the eighties quietly and humbly.

People magazine (1980) emphasizes Lennon the individual and structural family in its article titled, "In Praise of John Lennon: The Liverpool Lad as Musician, Husband, Father, and Man." The main body of the piece consists of excerpts from David Sheff's *Playboy* interview which was in the magazine on sale when Lennon was killed. In the one-page lead-in to the interview material, *People* ignored Lennon as symbol of the sixties and praised him for embarking "upon the most revolutionary undertaking of any rock star's career: an attempt to lead a normal life" (27). That attempt was "a bid for some measure of the security that had eluded him" (27). The focus is on Lennon's personal life—his lonely childhood, the isolation of fame, and his failed first marriage and estrangement from his first child. His "househusband" phase is noted for its emphasis on building a closer bond with his new child, Sean. The article also notes that Lennon turned over business responsibilities to Ono and that the move will guarantee "that his family will be free of the wrangling and litigation that has plagued the heirs of less foresighted rock greats" (27). *People*'s focus on matters of parenthood and good business sense reflects both its appeal to a broad audience and the increasingly different concerns of an aging sixties generation.

The portion of Sheff's interview that *People* printed focuses on Sheff's "day with the Lennons" in their seven-room apartment, one of five they owned in the Dakota. The picture is one of almost pure domesticity, with almost no links to the past. Sheff observes the apartment was "most notable for what it lacked; there was no guitar, no piano, not even a stereo system—no sign that a former Beatle or even a musician lived here" (29). The excerpt deals almost exclusively with John's relation to his five-year-old son Sean. Sheff quotes Lennon, "Sean is my biggest pride, you see. And you're talking to a guy who was not interested in children at all before" (30). Yoko says, "Most important is that we both work for the family now, and our family is our priority" (29). Sheff observes that young Sean's room is "the size of a small warehouse" and lists the playthings, which include a trampoline, a set of monkey bars, an assortment of huge stuffed animals, and a jukebox. Sheff notes that, despite the abundance of possessions, Sean does not seem spoiled, thus concluding with the suggestion that Lennon and Ono are indeed good parents.

In March 1981, *Ms.* magazine ran excerpts of an interview John and Yoko had with Dave Sholin of RKO radio on the very day Lennon was killed. *Ms.* titled the piece, "John and Yoko on Marriage, Children, and Their Generation." The editors' note thanks RKO for their permission to publish "John and Yoko's earnest—and heartrending—commitment to each other, their child, and their music" (58). A major portion of the interview excerpt is John describing a typical day in his present life and then offering some of his thoughts on child rearing. Lennon notes that he has to maintain an even keel emotionally as a father, that he can no longer afford to have "artistic depressions" (59). All along, Lennon attributes special prescience to his son and to all children. He says they "pick up on" adults' moods, and Lennon says if he starts getting depressed, "sure as hell, [Sean will] get a cold or trap his finger in a door" (59). Lennon's philosophy of child rearing as expressed in this interview is somewhat contradictory. Although he allows that he could not afford to be depressed around Sean, Lennon later says, "I think it's better for him to see me as I am. If I'm

grumpy, I'm grumpy. I try to be as straight with him as I can" (59).
Later he says "I'm tryin' to just have no real heavy discipline about
behavior" (59), but he goes on to list a number of things he demands,
which include eating and going to bed at regular times. Lennon expresses regret for his poor relationship with his first son, Julian, and
suggests that the boy has a right to be angry with Lennon because of
hypocrisy. "I learned a lot from a child because kids are not hypo-
crites and they're not phony. One does tend to fool oneself. And the
kids don't buy it" (59). In this interview Lennon reveals the kinds of
contradictions about child rearing that most parents can identify with,
but he also emphasizes an acute sensitivity to hypocrisy that characterized his own work and was one of the sixties generation's most
prominent criticisms of the dynamics of both the family and social
and political institutions.

LENNON AFTER THE BEATLES

Just as Jack Kroll, in his romantic evocation of sixties communitas, asserts that Lennon's best work is "locked up in the magic circle
of the 60's" (1980), writers expressing the reintegrative impulse struggle with pulling Lennon away from the sixties by emphasizing his
progress, and reversals, in the decade after the Beatles broke up and
the counterculture subsided.

Lawrence O'Toole, in a *Maclean's* piece titled "The Legacy of John
Lennon" (1980) focuses on Lennon's post-Beatle years. O'Toole begins by contrasting the generational identifications and hopes of Lennon's mourners with the later, reclusive Lennon who argued that his
fans exhibited a love–hate relationship with him; his fans, said Lennon, say "Thank you for everything you did for us in the '60s—would
you just give me another shot? Just one more miracle?" (37). O'Toole
focuses on Lennon's constant impulse to individuality, on his constantly
changing the rules for his fans. O'Toole praises his "willingness to
try every avenue open to self-realization and his willingness to admit
some of them were cul-de-sacs. He had the good sense not to fear
making a fool of himself, therefore experiencing no humiliation or
embarrassment" (36).

O'Toole views Lennon's five-year silence from 1976 to 1980 as an
exercise in integrity: "He didn't have anything to say. Unlike other
rock stars of his era who didn't have anything to say, but said it a
couple of times a year with new albums, Lennon would remain silent" (37). He also notes that Lennon was full of contradictions (39):

"The man who wrote 'Working-Class Hero' led a cushy, if confined life in the Dakota. An incisive and clear thinker, he nonetheless attributed magic powers to the Egyptian antiques he collected."

O'Toole values Lennon for his free spirit and willingness to experiment, and, instead of nostalgia for the lost sixties, he focuses on the "promise of a slightly different sort" in one of Lennon's last songs, "Starting Over"—the promise of the 1980s, which Lennon had hoped to communicate to (in Lennon's words) "the people who grew up with me" (39). This last quote from Lennon serves O'Toole well, for it says we all have grown up and warrants a focus on the present rather than the past. The promise of the eighties is quieter, more privatized. To realize it, O'Toole implies, is to have both the courage of our convictions and our indecisions. O'Toole presents an existential lesson in Lennon. The dream is dead, but we still must carry on in its absence, as Lennon said well before his death, "you must create your own dream." That is what it means, O'Toole suggests, to be survivors.

Los Angeles Times music critic Robert Hilburn (1980, 82) was moved to write not of Lennon's music but of his warmth. "Few people I've met in rock were as easy or as stimulating to be around," he remembered. What is interesting about Hilburn's piece is that he praises Lennon for what are generally considered to be adult attributes, things sixties youth might have scoffed at or even considered phony. Lennon, according to Hilburn was alway "gracious" and "he seemed to go out of his way to make people feel at home." The icon of a revolutionary counterculture is elegized in terms that suggest aspects of middle-class politeness.

Nationally syndicated columnist Ellen Goodman focuses on remembering Lennon in the context of the present, the context of growing older (1980) She recalls seeing a "Beatles booth" at an antique show recently and remarks that "it is always surprising when our youth becomes a collector's item." She saw Lennon's face again on the front page:

> But the Lennon I'll miss isn't the brilliant Beatle of the 1960s with his hair "rebelliously" grown below his ears. That Lennon exists on my records. The man I'll miss is the one I just met again, the man of the 1980s, moving in new ways, making new sounds. Five bullets wiped out this father, husband, musician—human work in progress.

Our sadness and sense of loss, Goodman emphasizes, should be directed not at the past—"You can't kill what a man has already done"—but the future—"Dammit, it's the promise that's gone." Noting that she is more the Beatles' age than their fans' ages, Goodman says she was moved by Lennon's emergence at age forty. His new record was "the work of a survivor." Lennon had survived fame and playing a role in which "other people were the directors"; he had survived business managers and pressures to keep pumping out music; and he had survived expectations to self-destruct "like Dylan Thomas or the rock stars with needle tracks up their arms." Lennon survived these assaultive expectations by "jumping into his private life as if it were a lifeboat" and by getting "in touch with the routines that root all of us with dailyness. He took care of his child instead of being taken care of like a child. He let himself go into new rhythms."

The notion of being taken care of like a child refers most pointedly to the pampered life of the celebrity, especially the rock star, but it suggests something about the sixties, too. The sixties generation, like Lennon, has to let go of being children, and they do not help themselves by mourning for the past in Lennon's death. The lesson, according to Goodman, is one of reintegration into those roots of "dailyness" and the "new rhthyms" of growth and change and responsibility.

Tony Kornheiser, in the *Washington Post* (1980), elegizes John Lennon as the Beatle "you'd most want to be" because he "spoke for your soul and your highest inspiration" and because "like Humpty Dumpty, he took the biggest falls." Kornheiser says Lennon really suffered and provided a lesson in the living of life. His life was characterized by commitment, whether it be to ideals of peace and love or, later, to his wife and child.

Tom Zito, in another *Washington Post* piece (1980), praises Lennon for his elasticity: "Sometimes he seemed like a chameleon: the workingman's hero he had sung about dressed in a tuxedo and mixing it up with the artsy types at a Kennedy Center gala." Zito recalls that when Lennon had to go to court he could put on a suit and "not act too witty on the witness stand," and he mixed with congressmen and carhops with equal ease. When Zito had wanted to interview him recently, Lennon expressed his sense of change and growth thusly: "We could do another interview but we did it nine years ago. We're neither of us really the same person, so why go back to where we were nine years ago. I've learned to raise children, and you've learned to write about things more cataclysmic than the next album by the Who Knows Whats. Wouldn't it be better to leave it that way. Let's have tea sometime."

Rock critic John Rockwell, in a piece in the *New York Times* (1980), calls Lennon "the most impassioned, and probably the most deeply talented of all the Beatles." But his piece also reminds members of the sixties generation that they and Lennon have grown older, perhaps too old to really be a part of rock and roll. Rockwell describes Lennon and McCartney's unique collaboration in creating music "that helped define a generation." Rockwell notes, though, that by the mid-sixties they really were writing their own songs, but they listed themselves as co-writers for reasons of legality and group cohesion. Lennon was more the rocker and had "the deepest and most convoluted sense of rock's anger and potential triumph." It was his roots in early rock and roll that caused him difficulty in the 1970s, according to Rockwell. During the post-Beatle time, Lennon tried to recapture the power of his youth, and "to reconcile it with his adulthood, but he had severe difficulties." None of the causes to which he directed his musical energy in the 1970s, including leftist politics, religion, and self-awareness, could match the passion and intensity he felt for basic rock and roll. Rockwell locates a major part of Lennon's creative core in a pre-sixties time.

Rock and roll, though, is the music of the young, and Rockwell evaluates Lennon's last album as simply an extension of the "domestic inversion" he had undertaken in his late 1970s househusband phase. The music of *Double Fantasy*, says Rockwell, is "a tired recycling of his youthful idioms—a sincere but slightly misguided fixation on domestic happiness that really doesn't suit rock at all." Yet Rockwell finds an appropriate irony in *Double Fantasy*, for Lennon had indeed remained a spokesman for his generation that had grown older; he was "as true in personal retreat as he had been in the joyful assertion and tortured protests of his earlier years."

LENNON AND YOKO ONO:
GROWTH AND TRANSFORMATION

Lennon and Yoko Ono's ideas about "creating" and "working on" a marriage and relationship were seen by some as reflecting the success of some of the sixties' messages that challenged traditional structural roles. Certainly the concept of "love" had shifted a long way from its ethereal status in the late 1960s. Love had to do, in 1980, with the more specific problems of a couple in their forties who tried to adjust new ideas to marriage, a basic structural form. Lennon and Ono's relationship became a microcosmic arena where sixties ideals were tested against the hard realities of aging and structure.

An initial step in this process was simply the ackowledgment of Yoko Ono, who had been at best ignored, at worst reviled, by Lennon fans and rock critics alike. A major focus of writings on Lennon and Ono had to do with their collaborative relationship in both art and life and with their attempts to forge an equal relationship. Lennon and Ono could be seen as a model for relationships that could adapt to the demands of the world of structure but also honor some of the old sixties ideals. Finally, their relationship could be seen as offering a corrective to the latent sexism in rock and roll and the counterculture.

In the wake of Lennon's death, Yoko Ono became the focus of public sympathy that contrasted starkly with the enduring resentment she had felt ever since coming into John Lennon's life. She had been seen as "the Dragon Lady" (Brownmiller 1981, 36), as "a distaff Svengali" who influenced Lennon's music in wrong ways and who was responsible for breaking up the Beatles (O'Toole 1980, 38). Lennon described the fans' reactions to his relationship with Ono as "this Japanese witch has made him crazy" (Sholin 1981, 63). Yoko Ono was resented, wrote Susan Brownmiller in *Rolling Stone*, for her "grim demeanor," for her "preposterously unfeminine" belief in her artistic talent, and for not fitting the popular stereotype of a rock superstar's foxy lady. Ono was seen, says Brownmiller, as "an abrasive outsider who . . . tried to break up [the Beatles] . . . a driving, impassive bitch with an unfathomable sexual hold on the sweet, working-class poet."

Ono remains a disturbing and difficult figure, and coming to terms with her, even in the context of collective, ritual grief, may lie beyond the capacity of some of Lennon's fans, says Brownmiller. Several weeks before Lennon's death, Ono had spoken of the long history of resentment by saying the hate she felt from the public kept her going, "When you're hated so much, you live. Hate was feeding me" (O'Toole 1980, 38). In the context of national mourning that the nation had rehearsed so well since 1963, Yoko Ono as grieving widow was idealized and did become an object of sympathy; more important, she became acknowledged as an important part of the "meaning" of John Lennon and the sixties.

In his *Los Angeles Times* (1980) piece, Robert Hilburn credited Ono as having been crucial to both Lennon's art and life. In Ono, Lennon had found someone as forceful and direct as he; they wanted to move forward and examine, and their give-and-take relationship allowed them to test various possibilities. Hilburn recalls that during his interview with Lennon just two months before his death, Lennon and Ono, "both spoke deeply of their need for each other. Lennon acknowledged that Yoko was even more important to him than his music."

Lawrence O'Toole in his elegy for Lennon in *Maclean's*, pays special tribute to Lennon and Ono's artistic collaboration. Lennon and Ono, says O'Toole, "became a force to be reckoned with . . . They produced a blush on the world's fair complexion . . . Yoko, who played the straight man, hardly ever smiled: John, with an alternately droll and sassy wit, did the original fool on the hill. They were playing high mass on a kazoo" (39).

In his second *Village Voice* piece (titled "Symbolic Comrades") on Lennon after his death, Robert Christgau focuses on Lennon's relationship with Ono (1981). Christgau reviews *Double Fantasy*, which in the elegies and reviews often was credited as being Lennon's last album, when it was in fact a collaborative effort between him and Ono. *Double Fantasy*, in Christgau's view, reflects a complex relationship between Lennon and Ono in which art and life could hardly be separated.

Christgau mentions the negative reviews of the album (some of which were pulled before publication after Lennon's death), but Christgau argues that the album was much better than critics believed. Despite the "simplistic words and less than adventurous music," the album reveals Lennon sounding good, and Christgau surmises that perhaps "the times had caught up with Yoko's singing." As for the album's meaning, Christgau says there is no doubt it was "John and Yoko's love album." Christgau emphasizes that their relationship was far from perfect and that, in the wake of Lennon's death, it has been sentimentalized into "an ideal marriage for the Age of Survival." Their relationship, he says, was rather neurotic, arguing that when Lennon sings a line like "the little child inside the man" he is describing correctly a significant aspect of his marriage. Citing other observers who suggested that Lennon had seemed infantilized by the time of his death, Christgau says Lennon's "matrifying mystification" of Ono is "basically sexist"; it suggests "the Earth Mother twaddle that has deradicalized so much of left-wing feminism."

But Christgau says we should not expect ideology from a rock star and that, for him at least, Lennon never was particularly convincing as an ideologue. The great gift that Yoko Ono gave to John Lennon, according to Christgau, was to shield him, as did the other Beatles, from the deep sense of aloneness that he dreaded. Shielded from this aloneness, Lennon could produce work that transformed the anger that lay beneath his surface into joy and hope. That, argues Christgau, was Lennon's great political value. And even if their marriage had its neurotic aspects, Christgau asks why we should insist that neurosis be defeated or escaped. The marriage allowed Lennon to turn his compulsions into art, and it was, indeed, a liberated marriage, with male and female roles convoluted. Their marriage was, says Christgau, "a saga of autotherapy with few parallels in our obsessively psychoanalytic culture. It was also a great romance." Christgau concludes that *Double Fantasy* is, from his standpoint as critic and fan, "gratifying," and he says, with, I suspect, a good deal of warmth, that "connubial rock and roll is hard to find."

Susan Brownmiller, in *Rolling Stone* (1981), made an observation similar to Christgau's when she offered that while Yoko Ono's own artwork has not been particularly convincing, "her true creative talent lay in nurturing John, in serving as his mother, his teacher, his guru, his senses, his master of zen." This seems a startling assertion coming from a staunch feminist such as Brownmiller, but she asks why such a situation should trouble us and why we cannot take Lennon at his word that Ono did indeed save his life and give him some measure of sanity, meaning, and love.

What may trouble us, Brownmiller suspects, is that Ono gave Lennon maternal love, which he was able then to both receive and give, in turn, to his own son. We may also be troubled that Ono was indeed a conduit from new ideas and causes to "John the dreamer," but Brownmiller reminds that this dependency, which many may find "scary," was always on public display. Ono got Lennon to understand the new ideas of the women's movement and to break through the sex-role stereotypes he had carried through his life. She suggests that Ono allowed John Lennon to discover his own maternal capacity. In Brownmiller's words, "Yoko Ono's greatest talent . . . her major conceptual work of art . . . her life's work was to take apart the broken pieces of John Lennon in stop-time motion and to put them back together again." Brownmiller notes that the longer they stayed together the more they began to look alike.[1] They seemed to be absorbing each other and melting into one. She suggests this blending confounded many. It struck at our preconceptions of gender roles and structural family roles. Whether it was neurotic or trendy, Brownmiller concludes that "it appears to have been wholly experienced and deeply felt." Brownmiller's and Christgau's pieces both suggest that Lennon and Ono may have provided a model for adapting new values to traditional structural relationships.

LENNON AND ONO AND SEXISM

Except for Susan Brownmiller, no woman wrote a major magazine essay on Lennon, and only a relative few wrote newspaper features and columns. Women were most conspicuous in photos and television images as mourners, weeping while holding flowers or singing "Give Peace a Chance." Women lent gravity and grace to the occasion by their steadfast, sincere presence, by their patient vigils outside the Dakota or in Central Park or anywhere else where the saddened sixties people gathered in the old spirit of tenderness and togetherness. They were generally excluded, though, from performing the various priestly tasks of elegizing the fallen leader of the tribe, primarily because so few were rock critics. They played supporting roles in this last great ritual as they had played supporting roles in rock and roll and in the sixties counterculture.

Nationally syndicated columnist Nicholas von Hoffman spent part of the 1967 "Summer of Love" in San Francisco's Haight-Ashbury district. His rich and sometimes acerbic account of hippie life (1968) includes the following observation:

> Hip or straight, the essential feminine role is intractably the same: the old ladies of the Haight do the cooking, the sewing, and the house cleaning like the young matrons in the suburbs. They walk one step behind their men, submissive, yet often retaining a ferocious protection of their idea of womanliness. The younger girls, the teenagers, don't seem to have the trait. They'll allow almost anything to be done to them. (203)

The fundamental rock-and-roll and counterculture values of impulse, irrationality, and immediate gratification are all much more problematic for girls than for boys. As Frith has observed, "The irrational elements of the counterculture—in other words, the sex and drugs and rock and roll—could not be appropriated by girls as they were by boys without affecting their self-definitions, their relationships, their lives" (1981, 243; see also Frith and McRobbie 1978–79). As Yoko Ono remarked in the Sholin interview in *Ms.* magazine, "In the sixties there was a sexual revolution, but it turned out to be a sexual revolution for men and not for women. And women started to feel very resentful and felt used" (Sholin 1981, 64). Two writings on Lennon and Ono's relationship addressed the fact of entrenched sexism in both rock and roll and the sixties counterculture by emphasizing John Lennon's struggles with his own sexism.

Susan Brownmiller observed that Yoko Ono "was the dangerous, uninvited female who walked into the clubhouse and demanded a change in the rules," and referring to charges that Ono was responsible for breaking up the Beatles, Brownmiller summarized the argument that Ono was "the evil schemer who put an end for all time to the song" (1981). The idea that Yoko Ono "broke up" the Beatles has to do, in part, with the Beatles as an embodiment of adolescent male fantasy—four young lads, suspended between childhood and adulthood, singing, playing, and living together surrounded by adoring girls. And Lennon did apparently live that kind of life in the early Beatle years, even though he was married and a father (Coleman 1984). The young Lennon was pugnacious with men and aggressive with women. He once severely beat a British disc jockey who accused him of homosexuality (Coleman, 189). Lennon's relationship with Yoko Ono, starting in 1968, was the beginning of a long and not always smooth journey toward feminism. He and Yoko specifically addressed this process in the Sholin interview published in *Ms*.

Ono and Lennon both agreed that he took a long time to change his attitudes. Lennon admitted he was only "intellectually" a feminist when he wrote and recorded "Woman Is the Nigger of the World" in 1972. Ono emphasized how far Lennon had come from his "archaic background" and his "macho" attitudes. Lennon, true to his penchant for generalizing from his own experience and ever aware of his role as a leader, pronounced that it was time we destroyed macho notions "because where has it gotten us all these thousands of years" (64). Do men have to arm wrestle each other and do they have to seduce women to prove they are men? he asked. And he characterized the present state of the world as "ninety-year-old men playing macho games with the world and possibly the galaxy" (Sholin 1981, 64). Lennon and Ono both agreed that "Starting Over," his hit song from *Double Fantasy*, was written not just to Ono but to all women. Lennon said as he was "starting over" with Ono, he hoped men would "start over" in their attitudes toward women. Lennon hearkened back to an old sixties catch word, but in a more focused way, when he said of the song, "It's a political song, I mean it's a love song but at the same time love is the only thing that is going to change this society—in the sense that love is a very powerful political weapon" (64). The words could have been spoken fifteen years earlier, but in 1980 they referred specifically to a realm of power relations largely neglected in sixties' rhetoric about equality and freedom. Lennon left no doubt about the changed context of his work at the end of the interview:

> I am not aiming at sixteen-year-olds. If they can dig it, please dig it. But when I was singing and writing this and working with her, I was vizualizing all the people of my age group in the sixties being in their thirties and forties now, just like me, and having wives and children and having gone through everything together. . . . The world is not like the sixties; the whole map's changed; and we're going into an unknown future, but we're still all here. While there's life. (Sholin 1981, 64)

Lennon had, just before his death, self-consciously positioned himself and his work as reflecting the life paths of the sixties generation, and, ever ambivalent about celebrity and leadership, he still offered up his own life as a possible example for moving forward into that "unknown future."

SEPARATING LENNON FROM COMMUNITAS

A significant move toward reintegration and ritual reentry to the social order had to do with members of the sixties generation letting go of John Lennon as a symbol of sixties communitas, as a repository of millions of individual hopes and dreams, and finally as a symbol of lost youth. These voices are, to some extent, responses to sixties nostalgia, because they propose that the John Lennon of 1980 himself rejected that nostalgia and looked forward to making sense of life in the times to come.

Lester Bangs, a writer-musician and counterculture veteran himself, lashes out in a *Los Angeles Times* piece (1980) at the "pathetic" people of his generation who "refuse to let their 1960s adolescence die a natural death," and he is even more scornful of "the younger ones who will snatch and gobble any shred, any scrap of a dream that someone declared over 10 years ago." Much mourning is self-centered, argues Bangs: "The Beatles were most of all a moment. . . . It is for that moment—not for John Lennon the man—that you are mourning, if you are mourning. Ultimately you are mourning for yourself." Arguing that Lennon "at his best despised cheap sentiment," Bangs attacks the rash of "gut curdling sanctimonies about ultimate icons." He believes that many are falsifying their memories of a "neverland 1960s that never really happened *that* way in the first place."

Such falsification, Bangs says, insults memories of the sixties as they happened. Bangs does not discount the experiences of the sixties; rather he questions reconstructions of communitas as he sees them played out in mass media and in mass gatherings. Bangs emphasizes Lennon's individuality and toughness, that "cynical, sneeringly sarcastic, witheringly witty and iconoclastic" John Lennon. Bangs's blunt message is that we do not have a collective dream, and we are better off accepting that fact than in trying to resurrect a dead personal dream. As we mourn our own lost pasts, we need to allow Lennon his individuality and free him, even in death, from our demands. Lennon was, in the end, "just a guy," but fans refused to ever let him be just that.

Dave Marsh, in his *Rolling Stone* (1981) essay titled "Ghoulish

Beatlemania," explores the notion that Lennon's death had something to do with his celebrity and with "our" particular relationship to him. Marsh directs anger at fans and the general condition of celebrity in contemporary American culture; he also criticizes his own role in that process. Marsh says "we" resented Lennon after he broke up the Beatles, and in our resentment we established a situation that led to his death: "Chapman thought he was eliminating a symbol, not murdering a man. Where did he get such an idea?" (1981, 29). Marsh points a finger at himself, admitting that in 1978 he wrote "An Open Letter to John Lennon" in *Rolling Stone* asking him to come out of retirement "and help make sense of events." Lennon's reply that he "didn't owe anybody anything" made Marsh feel small:

> Like most rock fans, I took it for granted that John Lennon existed to pump out entertainment, inspiration and insight. It never occurred to me, until then, that my attitude reduced someone I thought I loved and admired to the status of a vending machine. (28)

Marsh expresses outrage that the morning after the killing a promoter suggested an annual superstar benefit concert as a continuing memorial to Lennon. The promoter, according to Marsh, had been attempting for years to reunite the Beatles, and Marsh is angered that such promoting of Lennon as "John the Savior Beatle" perpetuates the conditions that led to his murder. By making "nagging demands" on Lennon and expecting him to explain or reconstruct the world for us, we differ from Chapman only in degree, argues Marsh. We reduce Lennon to a symbol and forget he was a person.[2]

For much of the 1980s Harry Stein, a contributing editor for *Esquire*, wrote an "Ethics" column for that magazine. In his piece on Lennon's death, titled "Oh, Grow Up!" (1981) Stein challenged nostalgic notions of the sixties as both harmful to individuals and demeaning to the memory of Lennon. Stein begins by noting a recent appearance of Jimmy Stewart on the *Tonight Show*. Stewart, says Stein, addressed himself to the subject of old age and physical deterioration with wit and guilelessness that "were nothing less than wonderful" (16). Stein muses on our cultural obsession with youth and notes that it has become more pronounced among the postwar generation. "Most of us," he observes, "in our late twenties and early thirties have adamantly refused to move past emotional adolescence. Forget about what it means to be sixty or seventy or eighty; some of us can't face what it means to be thirty-two" (16). This situation seems to result from the "seemingly permanent attatchment of our generation to the glory days of the sixties" (16). Stein says he knows more than a few people who confess to never having felt right about themselves since those days. He quotes an "extremely successful" independent producer who claims that he never thought those times would end and, in an evocation of communitas, laments, "I've been trying to re-create the kinds of emotional ties with people I had then" (16). Stein notes wryly that the producer seems to have succeeded, because none of his relations with the opposite sex has lasted more than six months.

Stein also proposes that another sign of our emotional adolescence is a continued predilection for self-destruction. He remembers sitting in a bar watching a televison report on the upswing of heroin use. One of the locals, much older than he, wondered why people do such things to themselves. Stein replied, "Kicks"—a concept foreign to the questioner. Drug use, says Stein, "may not be the most sensible behavior in the world, but we've been thoughtless for so long that it's almost second nature" (17). At the core of this adolescence, says Stein, is that "many of us are unable even to think of ourselves as adults" (17). We continue to define ourselves as kids. Stein suggests that the demographic force of the baby boom may have something to do with such insular perceptions.

John Lennon's death, he notes, has been played in the press as the end of our youth. But Stein says this "widespread sense of personal disorientation" is at odds with Lennon's own view of the world. Stein quotes Lennon from the October *Playboy* interview: "If the Beatles of the Sixties had a message it was to learn to swim. Period. And once you learn to swim, swim. The people who are hung up on the Beatles and the Sixties' dream missed the whole point when the Sixties' dream *became* the point" (18). Stein notes that Lennon's life was one of continual growth. While many of his followers wallowed in dreams and nostalgia, Lennon became capable of profound, enduring commitment. He ignored peer pressure and "came to understand that the only answers worth having are those one learns on one's own" (18). Stein points out that Lennon said of the Beatles 1967 mockingly ironic celebration of youth, "When I'm Sixty-Four," that it was Paul McCartney's song completely, that he would never dream of writing a song like that. No, Stein says, Lennon's dreams were different, and Stein says he cannot help believing "that John Lennon would have made every bit as terrific an old man as Jimmy Stewart" (18).

QUESTIONING LENNON AS POLITICAL SYMBOL

By 1980 much had happened in the fifteen or so years since the

youth movement had created a counterculture in the emotional cauldron of communitas. At that time, the counterculture was, in John
Leonard's words, a "self-ratifying community" (1980, 30). However,
two elegies from a New-Left perspective offered empathic critiques
of Lennon's work and the political and cultural legacies of the sixties
generation. Both call into question elements of communitas that characterize the mourning for Lennon and address the question of how
well Lennon's work and sixties communitas had provided a model for
living in the world.

Bernice Martin's piece in *Encounter* (1981), "Not Marx but Lennon," allows "that Lennon stood for something which struck a deep
and reverberating chord in our culture (mainly in the under-forties,
but perhaps more widely)." Lennon's death, she argues, brought out a
submerged "invisible politics" (49) because Lennon bridged a gap
between the pop mainstream and the protest politics of the late sixties and early seventies. She notes that the main focus of works on
Lennon produced in the five months since his death had been his solo
work and his life after the Beatles. She sees evidence of a grassroots
political response that shows Lennon to have been "the keeper of the
conscience of popular radicalism" (50). But this mix of political feeling revived in the wake of Lennon's death is personalized and inco-
herent. Martin argues that even Lennon's most political works, such
as "Working Class Hero," express only a vague discomfort with political conditions, a discomfort that may well coexist with, say, a dis-
like of trade unions in the spirit of individualism. Lennon's songs
appeal most deeply to conventional American values steeped in romantic individualism. Martin quotes all of Lennon's "Imagine" as an
example of a "deeply apolitical and classically utopian impulse" that
eliminates all historical dilemmas. The real question, she says, is just
how do we give peace a chance (51)?

In an elegy in *Center Magazine*, Todd Gitlin wrote that the Beatles
"were the repository for a hundred diverse dreams and seemed to represent the possibility that everyone's dreams could come true at once"
(1981, 4). Some hoped the Beatles would reunite and even lead the
tottering counterculture as they would find the right things to say amid
the confusion. Such dreams, Gitlin asserts, are only perishable commodities in mass culture. The burden of carrying dreams, not only for
those of the counterculture, but vast dreams from every niche and dark
crack in the culture, is too great. Those multitude of dreams embody
"too much desparate need and too little clarity about self in a media
floodlit society" (4). To summon love, as Lennon did, was also to

summon up "its demonic underside" (4). Gitlin says the counterculture dream, as evocative as it was, was "too delicate" for this world:

> Everyday there are children to raise, sexual skirmishes to be fought, problems of money, problems of meaning. Counterculture values, at odds with each other, spatter into the workaday world like cold water onto hot oil. When was the last time you saw a simple solution strolling into your life? (4)

Despite the failure of counterculture values and the nostalgic impulse of much that has been written and expressed in the wake of Lennon's death, Gitlin holds out the possibility that the vigils and mournings for Lennon might be harbingers of a longing for collective action. In the minds of some, he imagines, there remained the question of whether the forces of love and justice could come round once more (4).

PULLING LENNON OUT OF THE SIXTIES

Pete Hamill's long elegy in *New York* magazine (1980, 38–50) covers several bases, including paying homage to nostalgic memories of the sixties. His primary thrust, though, is to pull Lennon out of "the magic circle of the sixties" (Kroll 1980) and onto the larger stage of history. Having acknowledged communitas early in his essay, Hamill, in effect, jettisons the sixties a quarter of the way through his piece. Whatever meaning there is to be wrested from the tragedy lies elsewhere: in Lennon's life story, in his artistic drive, somewhere outside the dark and disappointing cloud of the sixties. The overly simplistic (as they seem to Hamill) dreams of the sixties cannot do justice to the complexity and contradictions of Lennon's life and his expression of that life in his art.

His section on Lennon's life is titled "Working Class Hero," and it goes back to the working-class roots of rock and roll. He pictures Lennon as driven by a desire to escape the dreary world of Liverpool. Hamill uses quotes from his own earlier conversations with Lennon to paint a picture of him as a working-class dreamer, who possessed talent and drive enough to realize his dreams. Lennon told Hamill how he used to sit in Liverpool and dream of America. "Who wouldn't," Lennon said, reminding the American of the special mythical pull of his country. America, Lennon told Hamill, was "Chuck Berry, Little Richard, and girls" (45).

Hamill alludes to Auden's famous phrase about Yeats; Lennon, he says, was "hurt into art." Lennon's sense of abandonment and loneliness in his childhood are, for Hamill, the primary subjects of Lennon's life and art. Yet Hamill leaves open the question of Lennon's ultimate artistic achievement. Of Lennon's post-Beatle work he says simply that Lennon made some good music, some bad, but that, true to his artistic bent, "he seemed to be pushing against the limits of the pop-music form itself" (50). Art was the dream that fueled him, but what Hamill offers us is Lennon at the time the dream was new and fresh, before it could be corrupted in its attainment.

Hamill remembers an individualistic Lennon, a fifties rocker who, in 1963, rejected advice to listen to Bob Dylan: "Give me Chuck Berry, give me Little Richard. Don't give me fancy crap. Crap. American folky intellectual crap" (39). Lennon admitted he really just wanted to play rock and roll and that, in some ways, the early days, before fame, in the sleazy beer joints in Hamburg were the best. Lennon, according to Hamill, wanted more than fame: "He wanted something else: a purer vision, a harder art, the solitude of the creator. He could never do that as a Beatle" (50). Hamill ends by recounting a Lennon concert he attended in 1972:

> He was all tangled up then in radical politics, a court case, hounded by the Nixon crowd and the immigration people. But there was a moment when he did what he had always wanted to do, and I wanted him to do it all night long. He stepped forward, a small smile on his face, and he started to sing "Hound Dog." (50)

Hamill's account does not, I believe, simply lift Lennon from the sixties and drop him into the nostalgic soup of the fifties. It runs deeper. Annie Gottlieb reports that some boomers view the sixties as a kind of origin myth of a new tribe (1987, 9). Hamill directly engages the mythical tyranny of the sixties. His elegy says, in effect, that we were not born in the sixties; we did not magically come to consciousness the moment we smoked our first joint, the moment we first marched against the war, or the moment we gazed sullenly out the window of the bus rolling toward the induction center. We all were born into earlier worlds of love and hurt. Like Lennon, we are driven by our own singular ambitions. What dreams we have run deep into American myth, and, ironically, it is a bright and troubled boy from Liverpool who instructs us in this connection. Our roots are deep in our own histories, our families, our towns, and cities. Our lives and ourselves are ongoing. The sixties were just a stop along the way.

UNCERTAIN REINTEGRATION

Robert Christgau, in his *Village Voice* piece (1981), expressed the fragmented nature of the discourse on Lennon's death which suggested real divisions among those who shared a love for, or at least a deep interest in, John Lennon:

> Here are those who've always regarded John as a symbolic comrade, there are those who've always regarded him as an actual leader. Here are those who've aged with him, and there those so young they revere him as the spirit of an Edenic prehistory. Here are those secretly relieved to put the quietus on the '60s, there those who hope somehow to revive them. Here are those who moon about all-you-need-is-love and give-peace-a-chance, there those who are reminded once again that "love doesn't stop bullets." Here are those who lament the Beatles as avatars of their faded youth, there those whose hearts go out to the wife and son that John the ex-Beatle left behind.

Christgau expresses well the intensely conflicted sense of generational identity observed in expressions of mourning for John Lennon. The "meaning" of John Lennon was as fractured as the "meaning" of the larger social order in redress. Writings on Lennon's death suggest a view of members of the sixties generation as initiates in a dreamlike ritual in the liminoid space of mass-mediated communitas. In the wake of that communitas, they returned variously to the world of structure. But there was no central core of meaning and form available to them. Their communitas was not liminal, as Victor Turner describes initiation rituals in the tribal societies that allow intitates to reintegrate into society (1982, 24); rather, it was open-ended, as are the much less clearly defined liminoid spaces of modern life (see Turner 1982, 53–59).

Yet the writings on Lennon also reveal the essential reflective and reflexive nature of redress. The sixties generation showed themselves to themselves and talked about how they saw themselves (Turner 1982, 75). The redressive phase, Turner emphasizes, is a liminal time when interpretations are constructed for events leading up to crisis. There is an indeterminate nature to redress, but Turner sees that indeterminancy not as negation, emptiness, or "absence of social being," but as potentiality. It may be envisioned as form taking shape against a background of indeterminancy (1982, 77). By early 1981, the meaning of John Lennon for the sixties generation was still in question, but there was no doubt that Lennon's death induced in this generation a process of self-awareness. Such rekindled awareness would coincide with increased "use" of the sixties in the broader public dialogue in the 1980s. By 1988, John Lennon would again become the focal point of a cultural debate, as the concept of "the sixties" became more politicized.

NOTES

1. "Yoko," said John, "is me in drag" (O'Toole 1980, 38).
2. Karen Foss (1983) analyzes the "advisory functions" of several eulogies for John Lennon and concludes that they urge fans to focus on the ideals Lennon espoused (peace and love) rather than on Lennon as a symbol.

Part Four

**Lennon and Generational Identity
in the Late 1980s**

Part Four

Culture and the Construction of Identity in the Schools

7

The 1988 Battle over the Memory of John Lennon

For about a year after Lennon's death, a ritualized mass-mediated space existed for a mostly self-absorbed dialogue among members of the sixties generation. The voices of separation "tried on" one of the possible ends of social drama, but there was no realistic possibility of the sixties generation separating from the larger society. Indeed, its weakened sense of generational identity was the impetus for the theme of the "death of the sixties" in the Lennon elegies. Separation was a fleeting response that briefly served to unify segment members in their grief and anger and to indulge feelings of nostalgia for their own lost youth, feelings of communitas, and their old, shared antagonisms.

Generation members were faced with existing in the conflicted social order, and resignation was an option for many. In Annie Gottlieb's *Do You Believe in Magic*, horror novelist Stephen King expresses a cynical sense of resignation shared by many of his generation:

> None of it [the sixties] seems real to me now, and I didn't believe half of it when it was going on. What comes up for me when I think about the Sixties is turning on "The Tonight Show" and seeing Robert Culp in a Nehru jacket and a peace medallion. . . . It all seemed so surface and very little substance. (Gottlieb 1987, 7)

Under such cynicism often lies a sense of self-protection, a sense of having been fooled and betrayed by the idealism of the period. The voices of resignation in elegies for John Lennon no doubt expressed how many members of the sixties generation had submerged their sixties identities and simply accepted the fragmented social conditions into which sixties communitas had dissolved. But voices of acceptance, or reintegration, sought a middle ground between the romantic nostalgia of separation and the cynicism of resignation. They explored how Lennon could be a model of change and transformation, but not repudiation, of sixties' ideals, how Lennon could be a model for moving back into structure and the social order.

As James Carey (1985) argues, two main aspects of social dislocation that characterize social drama are problems of identity and the relationship to the social order. The discourse just after Lennon's death is mostly a self-contained one focused on questions of generational identity; that is, it is composed mostly of self-proclaimed generational voices speaking mostly to others in the segment. Evidence of social drama exists more clearly in the 1988 controversy that erupted with the publication of Albert Goldman's biography. Here we see more open conflict between the sixties generation and other segments, and generational discourse turns more specifically toward considering the generation's place in the social whole and the extent to which the generation will contribute to redefining the social whole and the meaning system that has been weakened in the process of social drama.

The central issue in the conflict over Albert Goldman's biography of John Lennon and in the general cultural context of sixties bashing in the 1980s is that of how the sixties are to be remembered in the 1980s and beyond. If John Lennon was, as Goldman asserts, a poor husband and father and a hopeless drug addict, then a symbolic model for reintegration is challenged. In the image of the transformed, adult John Lennon the generation could see how its past immersion in drugs and disorder could be either overcome or, even better, utilized and built upon to strengthen and deepen the performance of structural roles such as husband and father.

The John Lennon depicted by Albert Goldman, however, appears to be just another victim of what conservative voices of the 1980s characterized as the destructive permissiveness of the sixties. Both Lennon and the sixties counterculture stand discredited. If the group is seen, and sees itself, as being totally discredited, then reintegration would seem to require an open rejection of sixties identity. It would require a kind of "born again" conversion from error to enlightenment. It would mean an obliteration of sixties identity coordinates. Reentry into the social order would then be on terms dictated to the sixties generation by others, most prominently the voices of the conservative cultural and political revolution of the 1980s. The stakes involved in the 1988 controversy are those fundamental to social drama—identity, in this case cultural/historical identity, and the counterculture's sense of place in the social order.

GOLDMAN AND ONO: CHARGE AND COUNTERCHARGE

GOLDMAN'S CHALLENGE TO GENERATIONAL IDENTITY

Elegies for John Lennon that constructed messages of acceptance and reintegration for the sixties generation focused mostly on Lennon as a living symbol for the generation. In Lennon's later life, the generation could find implied models for ways to retain some of their earlier idealism and generational identities yet adapt to the realities of growing older in a changed social situation. Albert Goldman's 1988 biography of Lennon, *The Lives of John Lennon*, directly challenged this reintegrative view of Lennon. Goldman found fault with Lennon in almost all facets of his life, but perhaps most significant for the sixties generation was Goldman's debunking of accepted notions that Lennon "grew" in the 1970s. The book posited, instead, that Lennon had no sense of himself and that the image of his growth, culminating in his devotion to his son in his "househusband phase," in his deeper understanding of feminism, and in the soft domesticity of his final album, *Double Fantasy*, was a deliberately constructed fraud orchestrated by both Lennon and Yoko Ono. The "real" John Lennon, says Goldman, was hopelessly dependent on drugs: "John Lennon's drug addiction was the substance, the tissue of his life. It was as important to him as anything" (Kozinn 1988a, III: 15).

The book sparked a lively and often self-interested debate. The primary conflict was between Goldman and Yoko Ono, who set in motion a book and film on Lennon that appeared within weeks of the publication of Goldman's book. Around this primary conflict arose a periphery discourse of reviews and commentary in the popular national press. *Newsweek* accorded cover story status to the conflict, observing that the fight over the memory of John Lennon was fundamentally a battle over how a generation wished to view its history. The appearance of this conflict almost eight years after Lennon's death gives evidence that Lennon was a complex cultural figure, that he was still the most comprehensive and powerful cultural symbol for the sixties generation, and that he remained a cornerstone in the construction of meaning for both the sixties generation and other societal segments.

A REVIEW OF *THE LIVES OF JOHN LENNON*

Albert Goldman, a former English professor at Columbia University, had written about popular music and popular culture in the late 1960s for publications such as *Life, Esquire,* and the *New Leader.* He published a collection of his essays on rock music and jazz titled *Freakshow* (1971). In 1974 Goldman published a biography of the controversial comic, Lenny Bruce. It focused on Bruce's drug use and messy personal life. Goldman's 1981 biography of Elvis Presley, *Elvis,* became a bestseller. It focused largely on prurient details of Presley's descent into drugs and decadence. Goldman made over $2 million for *Elvis* and received a $750,000 advance from William Morrow for his Lennon biography. Goldman spent over six years on the Lennon project and interviewed some 1,200 friends, relatives, and associates of Lennon. Those closest to Lennon, though, refused to talk to Goldman. Ringo Starr and George Harrison declined interviews, and Paul McCartney refused Goldman specifically because he resented his treatment of Elvis Presley. Yoko Ono, Cynthia Lennon, and Julian Lennon also did not talk with Goldman. Goldman claims he began the Lennon biography with an open mind, with even a reverence for Lennon. He said that before the project he felt that "John Lennon was my idol in the rock world. He was someone of great intelligence and courage—the opposite of Elvis" (Kozinn 1988a). Goldman claims to have been disappointed by the material he uncovered.

The blurb on the back cover of the paperback edition of *The Lives of John Lennon* (1989) promises a study of a "turbulent personality of labyrinthine complexity." Lennon was "a man of a thousand faces" who enjoyed a gifted and inspired life but who privately lived in torment. The blurb concludes that "*The Lives of John Lennon* is a tribute to his legendary achievements and a revelation of the true price he paid for them." The blurb seems designed to attract anyone the least bit sympathetic to Lennon and promises a complex treatment of the subject. The book delivers something much different.

The Lives of John Lennon chronicles Lennon's life from childhood, but the primary focus is on Lennon's post-Beatle years, about which comparatively little had been written. Goldman advances a psychological theme centered around identity: that Lennon's traumatic childhood, when he felt abandoned by his mother, left him a legacy of rage and an unstable sense of himself, which propelled him on a lifelong search for a mother figure and constantly toward the comforts of infantile regression. Into this ample thematic vessel, Goldman pours a large volume of vilification.

His list of charges against Lennon is long and impressive. Lennon was prone to violent rages. He kicked Yoko in the stomach while she was pregnant and may have caused her to miscarry. He nearly battered a Liverpool disc jockey to death with a shovel. He threw a brick through Paul McCartney's window, and another time pulled one of his own paintings off McCartney's wall and put his foot through it. Lennon may have killed two people during the Beatles' stay in Hamburg, Germany, in the early 1960s. Lennon was cruel and sexist with women. He abused groupies and urinated on a nun. He once walked up to several women on the street in New York and asked them to perform a sex act. Lennon had a homosexual relationshipwith the Beatles' original manager, Brian Epstein, and was bisexual. During his supposedly tranquil "househusband phase," Lennon was actually a Howard Hughes–type recluse. Fearful and anorexic, he spent most of his time in bed in a darkened room using a variety of drugs, and he had little to do with his young son. Yoko Ono became so disgusted with him that she had made plans to divorce him. She ran their lives and manipulated Lennon to advance her own ambitions. She tipped police that Paul McCartney was entering Japan with drugs, and he was subsequently arrested. In addition to his personal failings, Lennon had significant artistic ones. He was a mediocre guitar player and the much-vaunted punning and wordplay in his lyrics may have come simply from a case of dyslexia.

If readers do not recognize the John Lennon on Goldman's pages, Goldman most succinctly explains why about two-thirds of the way through the book:

> When John was with the street people, he was the epitome of the street, just as when he was with Marshall McLuhan he was the epitome of the pop pundit, or with Pierre Trudeau, the epitome of the peace politician. Interview a score of people who interacted strongly with Lennon and you will get a score of Lennons, each one a man highly congenial to your source. Clearly, John took his identity from the company he kept. Thus the real John Lennon was only as real as his latest infatuation and always a man who was up for grabs. (1988, 599)

Goldman's Lennon is without a self, without a center, and everything he said or stood for is to be questioned in light of that.

The Lives of John Lennon opens with a scene supposedly from 1979. A "runner" brings a packet of heroin to Yoko Ono at the Dakota Apartments:

> Like a Zen arrow flying through the night, Kit Carter comes winging up Central Park West in the predawn darkness of a December morning in 1979. When he reaches the intersection of 72nd Street, he glances up at the Dakota, glimmering dimly in the light of a solitary streetlamp, like a ghostly German castle. Darting across the street to the iron portcullis guarding the tunnel-like carriage entrance, he gives the night

bell a short, sharp jab. Shuffling restlessly in the chill wind off the park, he waits for the doorman to emerge from the wood-and-glass windbreak surrounding the building's recessed entrance. As soon as the gate lock is snapped, Kit slips through and bounds up the steps to the concierge's office, where he exchanges a perfunctory nod with the night man before plunging into the maze of passageways that leads to the tall oak door of Studio One, the official office of Yoko Ono. (1988, 1)

Two pages later Goldman describes John Lennon waking up:

John Lennon comes to consciousness before dawn in a pool of light cast by two spots above the polished dark wood of his church-pew head-board. These lights are never extinguished because John has a horror of waking in a dark bedroom. Darkness to him is death. The first thing he looks for with his feeble eyes are the fuzzy red reflections in the big oval mirror above his bed. These smudges assure him that his life-sup-port system is working, for night and day he lives buffered by its sooth-ing sounds and flickering images, like a patient in a quiet room. (1988, 3)

What purports to be a biography begins with the feel of modern pulp fiction, with a heavily adjectival style that leaves little to the imagination. We seem ushered into an old fashioned tale that we surely have heard before. It is a tale of mystery, intrigue, and perhaps even horror. The Dakota is a dark castle. The king and queen are well hid-den from their unsuspecting, ever obeisant subjects. In their darkness and isolation, they descend into sloth, decadence, and deceit. It is also a "king has no clothes story," and Goldman makes the point literally by describing Lennon appearing stark naked in front of Yoko and Sean's nanny. Lennon apparently walks about the apartment like that "without a thought for whom he may meet, male or female, friend or stranger." He sits that way in the kitchen pontificating to the nanny, an exercise Goldman calls "the Naked Professor's lecture" (1988, 14). Amid this darkness and disorder, the young child runs around unre-strained, neither parent paying attention to his "feral antics" (11).

Goldman goes for the jugular of both the Lennons and the sixties generation in a dramatic refutation of the last happy image of Lennon presented in the media just before and just after his death. In the wake of Lennon's death, those who did not really know his work or did not identify with him or the sixties zeitgeist, offered at least a grudging concession that, whatever his failings and mistakes, Lennon was frank with his opinions and his life (compare Greenfield 1980; Rabinowitz 1981). Goldman begins by blasting even that small tribute. His is one of a number of voices in the late 1980s that vilifies sixties "permis-siveness" and the sixties generation.

KEEPING THE FLAME:
ONO'S BIOGRAPHICAL PACKAGE

The movie *Imagine: John Lennon* premiered in New York City on October 7, 1988. It was preceded by two other marketing tie-ins, a two-album soundtrack and a "coffee table" book made up of text and pictures from the film (Solt and Egan 1988). Yoko Ono was aware that Albert Goldman was doing a biography of Lennon almost from the start of the project, and she suspected that it would not be kind to his memory. In 1986, Ono approached noted documentary producer David Wolper about doing a film on the life of John Lennon. An experienced, mainstream producer, Wolper's previous credits included "The Making of the President: 1960," "The Rise and Fall of the Third Reich," a seventy-eight-program television series shown on PBS titled "Biography," and a documentary on Elvis Presley titled "This is Elvis." More recently, Wolper had produced films on the 1984 Olympics and the Statue of Liberty celebration. Ono provided Wolper and his director Andrew Solt over 200 hours of film and videotape from her private collection; she also provided some of Lennon's unreleased audio tapes. The film was ready for release just weeks after the publication of Goldman's *The Lives of John Lennon*. When asked about the timing Ono said, "It's such a beautiful coincidence" (Rense 1988, VI: 3). Director Andrew Solt, responding to the same question, expressed concern that the timing might lead some to view the movie as a "whitewash" response to the book (ibid.).

The 110-minute film covers all of Lennon's life and career, though it is centered around a period in 1971 when Lennon was making his acclaimed *Imagine* album at his and Ono's country estate at Tittenhurst, England. There is footage from the days of Beatlemania, including Lennon's famous remark at the Royal Variety performance in 1963, which was attended by the Royal Family—"Would the people in the cheaper seats clap your hands, and the rest of you just rattle your jewelry?" The Beatles producer George Martin provides illuminating commentary on the technical aspects of *Sergeant Pepper's Lonely Hearts Club Band*. The film emphasizes Lennon's post-Beatle years and his collaborations with Ono. One segment shows Ono in the recording studio instructing a technician on how she would like Lennon to sound on "Oh, Yoko."

There are scenes from the Montreal "bed-in for peace," including a confrontation with conservative cartoonist Al Capp in which "[John and Yoko] never looked saner" ("John Lennon: The Battle . . . ," 1988, 66). There is copious footage of John playing with his son, Sean; some of it accompanied by Lennon singing "Beautiful Boy," a song about Sean from Lennon's last album. There is no narrative, only recorded voices, mostly Lennon's. Other voices include those of Yoko Ono, Cynthia Lennon, and Julian Lennon. Producer David Wolper remarked that there probably was more personal footage shot on Lennon than on any other famous person who ever lived. "There were periods when he had a camera following him around for weeks," said Wolper (Kozinn 1988b, 19).

Imagine: John Lennon does seem to be an official counterdocument to *The Lives of John Lennon*. It is likely that news of Goldman's accusations leaked out at intervals during his research and writing and that Ono knew the Lennon image was, in fact, vulnerable on several fronts. Goldman, it was feared, would reveal situations, remarks, and actions that were essentially true, so the task for Lennon's defenders was twofold: emphasize the positive about John Lennon and discredit Goldman. The first task was effected by the movie and book, *Imagine: John Lennon*. The second task fell largely to *Rolling Stone* magazine, whose publisher, Jann Wenner, had had a long relationship with Lennon and Ono. The book *Imagine: John Lennon* (Solt and Egan 1988) provides an extra line of commentary compared with the film because the photographs have captions. The direct quotes that were heard in the film and in the captions reveal fairly obvious counters to Goldman.

One point of contention between Goldman and Ono has to do with one of the original members of the Beatles, Stu Sutcliffe, who left the group in 1961 to pursue a career in art. In 1962 he died of a brain tumor. Goldman reports that the Lennon housekeeper at the Dakota told him that Yoko Ono told her that John had always felt responsible for Stu's death because he thought he had kicked him in the head in a fight a year earlier. Goldman writes, "the death of Stu Sutcliffe haunted Lennon for the rest of his life" (1988, 137). But photographs in *Imagine: John Lennon* show the Beatles with Stu Sutcliffe in Hamburg, Germany. The last part of the caption states, "though Stu left the group, choosing to stay in Hamburg and study art, he and John remained good friends. In April 1962, Stu died suddenly of a brain tumor. Aunt Mimi later observed that Stu's death was 'one of the greatest blows of John's life'" (Solt and Egan, 41). Lennon is shown to grieve over Sutcliffe's death, and there is no suggestion of any incident that might engender remorse.

Goldman provides many details of Lennon's separation from Yoko Ono for eighteen months in 1973–74, which has come to be known as Lennon's "lost weekend." Goldman portrays Lennon during this period as almost perpetually drunk, violent, and abusive and often making a fool of himself by causing numerous embarrassing "scenes" in Los Angeles clubs and bars. Most of the time he was with his mistress, May Pang, a relationship undertaken apparently with the approval of Yoko Ono. This situation has been verified by more sympathetic biographers (compare Coleman 1984). *Imagine: John Lennon* does not ignore this period. It shows a photo of Lennon in the act of being ejected from a nightclub. The caption explaining the photo is preceded, though, by a caption for another photo of a pensive Lennon, which asserts that this was an extremely creative time for Lennon. He recorded three albums and produced another. The lead-in to the caption of the ejection photo reads, "Creativity, however, did not preclude drinking bouts. In March of 1974, he was roughly ejected from Los Angeles' Troubador Club after heckling the Smothers Brothers comedy team" (Solt and Egan, 184). The text suggests that Lennon's debauchery is perhaps somewhat mitigated by his creative production; Lennon is portrayed implicitly as the moody genius as opposed to Goldman's picture of the pitiful, abusive, insecure drunk.

In another caption May Pang is described as Lennon's "constant companion . . . who had worked for John and Yoko as a personal assistant" (Solt and Egan, 181). Pang had written a book about her well-known physical relationship with Lennon (Pang and Edwards, *Loving John*, 1983), but *Imagine: John Lennon* leaves the audience guessing as to their relationship. It also portrays "the lost weekend" as a transition period when Lennon grew up and accepted the responsibilities of adulthood. Long-time friend Elliot Mintz is quoted to that effect: "It was his departure from his youth, to becoming a man, to wanting to be with Yoko, to having a child" (Solt and Egan, 184). Lennon is quoted that the period was a "necessity" for him and Yoko to make a decision to "have a baby and seek fulfillment" (183). Lennon, said Elliot Mintz, had to prove that he was "worthy" of Yoko. The "lost weekend" almost takes on the aura of a mythical quest or initiation rite whereby the seeker emerges from a dark night of the soul. A potentially damaging situation is therefore turned to advantage as bad behavior is made to serve a theme of growth and transition.

Perhaps the most crucial task for the film *Imagine: John Lennon* was to counter the dark and disturbing picture Goldman had painted of Lennon's last years: the portrait of a crumbling, deceitful marriage; of a drugged and feeble Lennon who neglected his child and allowed himself to be manipulated by a scheming, ungrateful wife. The final scenes of *Imagine: John Lennon* depict Lennon as an energetic and doting father not only to his new son, Sean, but also to his first son, Julian, whom Goldman charges John had cruelly neglected throughout his life.

The caption under a photo of John holding his infant son says that after the boy was born "John turned all his attention to raising Sean, overseeing every detail" (Solt and Egan, 195). Another photo shows Lennon's first son, Julian, lifting baby Sean high into the air. The caption says that Julian visited John often and that they "began to develop a deeper relationship." It also suggests that a large-scale healing process had begun for John, who "also made peace with his own father [who had abandoned him] during this time" (196).

The Lennons made several trips to Japan in the late 1970s. They visited Yoko Ono's family and toured. Goldman makes the type of accusation about these trips that lends credence to charges that his work is simply mean-spirited. He asserts that during the visits to Japan and the East Lennon did not seem interested in anything cultural or artistic; that he instead preferred shopping, playgrounds, and amusement parks. But even so small a detail in Goldman is countered in *Imagine: John Lennon*. A caption reads, "While in Japan John immersed himself in the culture and, with Yoko and Sean, would often visit Buddhist temples where they prayed and meditated" (Solt and Egan, 207). Goldman also reports that Yoko's relationship with her family was strained during the time. *Imagine: John Lennon* displays a two-page photo of John, Yoko, and Sean plopped down in the middle of about fifty members of the Ono extended family, most of whom are smiling (208–9).

Goldman's portrayal of John and Yoko's deteriorating relationship and her domination of Lennon is challenged in a quote from John who says that nobody controls him, that he is the only person who can control him:

> For all you folks out there who think that I'm having the wool pulled over my eyes, well, that's an insult to me. But if you think you know me, or you have some part of me because of the music, and then you think I'm being controlled like a dog on a leash because I do things with her, then screw you, brother or sister, you don't know what's happening. (Solt and Egan, 213)

Lennon and Ono reaffirm their commitment to each other in quotes at the end of the book. Discussing his partnership with Ono in making *Double Fantasy*, Lennon says, "I wouldn't have worked without her . . . we're presenting ourselves as man and wife and not as sexual objects who sing love songs and are available to the audience. We're presenting ourselves as a couple, and to work with your best friend is a joy" (229). Lennon's statement here situates him and Ono very strongly in the adult phase of life that was celebrated in many 1980 elegies. Lennon rejects the old mode of youthful stardom with the ever-present groupies or having to present himself as a sex symbol. In keeping with the spirit of the reintegrative discourse for the sixties generation, Lennon shows that one can adapt to adulthood in new ways such as "connubial rock and roll," as Robert Christgau (1981b, 32) fondly dubbed *Double Fantasy.* Ono says that during the making of *Double Fantasy,* "We were like teenagers, falling in love again" (Solt and Egan, 229).

Ono's final tribute to Lennon is poignant both in print and on film. She says of him, "He was my husband. He was my lover. He was my friend. And he was an old soldier who fought with me" (231). Despite its propagandistic aspects, *Imagine: John Lennon* was widely regarded as an effective, even powerful, evocation of the memory of John Lennon.

ROLLING STONE'S ATTACK ON GOLDMAN

One critic described *Rolling Stone* magazine as "the house organ of the Lennon publicity machine" (Ferguson 1988). The relationship between *Rolling Stone* publisher Jann Wenner and John Lennon and Yoko Ono is a long and complicated one (see Draper 1990) The first issue of *Rolling Stone* in 1967 featured John Lennon on the cover; Lennon had encouraged Wenner in his new enterprise and provided him with valuable contacts in the music and entertainment world. By 1969 Wenner and his wife were socializing with John and Yoko. In 1970 Lennon gave Wenner a long interview that has now become oft-quoted. In it he said the Beatles and the sixties were over and that it was time to move on to new things. Lennon became angry with Wenner, however, for publishing the magazine interview later in book form. He and Wenner were estranged until Lennon's death. Despite Wenner and Lennon's personal disagreements, Wenner supported *Rolling Stone*'s criticism of the U.S. government for trying to deport Lennon. In 1980, Lennon, or at least a Lennon representative, approached Wenner just before the release of *Double Fantasy.* Lennon and Ono both were out on the interview circuit to promote the album, and an interview with *Rolling Stone* was arranged. Editors were disappointed with the interview not only because Lennon denounced Wenner but also because they simply did not find it interesting. Also, record reviewer Stephen Holden had written a lukewarm review of the album. Editorial decisions were being made on December 8, 1980, when Lennon died.

Wenner seemed genuinely grief stricken, and within hours of the announcement of Lennon's death he reportedly took a cab to the Dakota and stood outside with other mourners for several hours. The next day *Rolling Stone* began preparing its John Lennon memorial issue (January 21, 1981). The Lennon interview was trimmed of its references to Wenner, and the less-than-enthusiastic review of *Double Fantasy* was rewritten in a more properly elegaic spirit. *Rolling Stone* made itself a focal point for generational grieving for Lennon. The Lennon memorial issue sold a record 1.45 million copies, but *Rolling Stone* historian Robert Draper does not speculate on the sincerity of Wenner's motives. Draper notes that, like Hugh Hefner, Wenner had the knack for turning his personal obsessions into commercial success (1990, 60). After Lennon's death Wenner maintained a close relationship with Yoko Ono. They socialized, and *Rolling Stone* published an account of her trip to the Soviet Union in 1986; Wenner and his wife accompanied Ono on that trip (Draper 1990, 331 and 351; "John Lennon: The Battle . . . ," 1988, 68).

In 1988 *Rolling Stone* sprang quickly to Lennon's defense, running a cover story on Lennon in the October 20 issue, a little over a month after the publication of *The Lives of John Lennon.*

Rolling Stone may well have anticipated controversy over Goldman's book, for it ran what appear to be four separate lead-in stories. The first, in June 1987, was a remembrance of Lennon's first major concert appearance after the break-up of the Beatles (Fricke, "John Lennon and the Plastic Ono Band"). The article asserts that Lennon's hastily arranged appearance at a concert in Toronto in 1969 was "a major turning point in Lennon's career." Here, according to the article, Lennon declared his independence from the Beatles, and the performance captured Lennon's "raw honesty" at a time he "was anxious to shed his pop-idol skin." The article mentions that Lennon initially refused pay for the performance, but did finally accept $250, union scale, and he signed a Toronto musicians' union contract. The piece emphasizes qualities that Goldman would call into question—Lennon's honesty, charity, humility, and his special sixties form of authenticity, namely renouncing his pop-idol status and showing solidarity with the union. Here he is shown foreshadowing his brief, early 1970s persona as a working-class hero. The article also mentions that Lennon and Ono performed at several benefit concerts for various social and political causes during this period.

Later in the year, *Rolling Stone* published David Fricke's interview with Yoko Ono. The appearance of this interview suggests a campaign anticipating Goldman's book, since there was no apparent reason for featuring Ono at this time; the interview rather broadly deals with Lennon and Ono's political awareness through the years. Fricke goes to great lengths to frame questions for Yoko in order to elicit a certain type of response. For example, Fricke does not ask, "What in your experience has influenced your outlook on world peace?" Instead he asks, "How did growing up in Japan in the shadow of war and the atomic catastrophes at Hiroshima and Nagasaki affect your outlook on prospects for world peace?" The questions generally allow Ono to offer a chronicle of her and Lennon's contributions to making a better world.

At one point she credits Lennon with saving lives at the 1969 People's Park protests in Berkeley. Ono and Lennon were in Montreal at the time, and Lennon got a call from some of the protestors who asked, in Ono's words, "What shall we do, John?" Lennon advised them, reports Ono, not to confront the police, "to survive first." Ono's perspective on that particular conflict is that "in a way we did win," because that park area now is green and beautiful. One truly amusing part of the interview is when Fricke asks a question that, I suspect, could only be understood and appreciated by those who lived through the sixties. Returning to his original world-peace theme, Fricke asks Ono, "It's been twenty years since you stood in a bag in Trafalgar Square for peace. What do you feel are the realistic prospects for world peace?" Ono replies that she thinks we'll survive. "There's plenty for all of us in the world. It's just a matter of distribution," says the woman who sold a cow for $250,000.[1]

Rolling Stone announced the making of the film *Imagine: John Lennon* on June 2, 1988, four months before its release (Ressner, "Lennon film . . . ," 23). The short piece noted that its premiere was set to coincide with Lennon's forty-eighth birthday. The article used a quote that would later become a staple in the publicity campaign. Producer David Wolper said he was not familiar with Lennon's music and politics and asked Ono why she picked him to do the documentary. According to Wolper, Ono said, "Because I need somebody strong that I can't push around." Wolper also says the documentary shows glimpses of "Lennon's angry sides . . . offering audiences a truthful portrait."

Finally, just before the release of the film, *Rolling Stone* ran a short article titled "The Making of 'Imagine'" (Ressner 1988, 37) consisting of inteviews with Wolper and Solt that conveyed generally what would become the "official" version of the genesis and meaning of the project. Its main points were: Ono approached Wolper after much soul searching; Wolper and Solt felt overwhelmed by the 200 hours of film and videos provided by Ono, a detail suggesting perhaps that this version of Lennon's life is compiled from a huge cache of empirical evidence; Wolper and Solt explain that by using mostly voiceovers from Lennon rather than a narrator, they were giving Lennon "a chance to speak for himself"; and Wolper and Solt deny that the film and book are in any way a reply to Goldman.

The *Rolling Stone* rebuttal to Goldman was published on October 20, 1988. David Fricke and Jeffrey Ressner begin their article with an anecdote. They refer to a Los Angeles disc jockey who has been getting calls from fifteen- and sixteen-year-old girls who are upset over the allegations about Lennon in Goldman's book. The younsters ask the disc jockey if that is what John Lennon really was like. Fricke and Ressner imply not only that Goldman's biography assassinates the character of John Lennon but that it also has traumatized this younger generation of rock fans. The refutation of Goldman thus takes on the aura of a noble task—to bring truth to the children. This dramatic setting suggests themes of innocence and betrayal central to the experience of the sixties generation. As adults lied to children about Vietnam and racism in the sixties, now an adult, an "other," lies to this generation of children, the children of the sixties people, about a sacred icon. The refutation of Goldman thus takes on elements of the sixties generation's sense of their own unique history and experience, and it appeals simultaneously to their possible structured situations as protectors of children, whether the children are real biological offspring or the next generation of rock fans.

Fricke and Ressner announce that their "intensive investigation" of *The Lives of John Lennon* reveals that the book "is riddled with factual inaccuracies, embroidered accounts of true events that border on fiction and suspect information provided by tainted sources" (1988, 43). Several of Goldman's sources, say the authors, claim to have been misquoted or that Goldman twisted information they gave him.

The article does admit that some of Goldman's charges are valid. The authors do not deny Goldman's claim that *Rolling Stone* has had "an obvious connection" with Lennon and Ono over the years. The authors counter only that *Rolling Stone* also published excerpts from Goldman's biography of Elvis Presley in 1981. The authors note also that Ono admits she was using heroin in 1979, as Goldman describes in the opening of his book. Of this assertion, Fricke and Ressner allow that Goldman "comes within striking distance of the truth" (1988, 52). They refer to the heroin use, in terms Ono used, as a "problem." They assert though that, contrary to Goldman's claims, Lennon knew about "the problem" and that Ono was off heroin before they began recording *Double Fantasy.* The authors step back at one point and concede that "there is much about John Lennon in Goldman's book that is true—that he took drugs, that he was obsessed with his mother, Julia, that he feuded with Paul McCartney, that he was self-destructive" (1988, 48). But, rejoin the authors, all of that "is hardly news," for it had been documented in previous books (compare Coleman 1984, Green 1983; Pang and Edwards 1983), and Lennon himself had talked and written songs about all of it.

Fricke and Ressner focus most of their attack on the credibility of two sources who provided some of the more damning charges. Marnie Hair, the mother of one of Sean's playmates, claims she was close with the Lennons in the late 1970s. Ono denies it. Goldman's picture of a dissolute Lennon and Ono in the Dakota is based largely on Hair's accounts, but Goldman did not reveal, Fricke and Ressner note, that Hair also had filed a large lawsuit against Ono about an injury to her child on Ono's property. Fred Seaman was another of Goldman's questionable sources who provided information on the "Dakota years." Goldman does not mention that Seaman stole Lennon's personal diaries after Lennon died and that he was convicted of theft in the case and sentenced to five years' probation. (The paperback edition [1989], published after the *Rolling Stone* article, does mention these facts in a final section on sources.)

In a couple of instances, Fricke and Ressner resort to tactics similar to those for which they criticize Goldman. They report that Lennon's pal during "the lost weekend," singer and composer Harry Nilsson, says Goldman tried to get him drunk and pump him for information. Goldman, however, got drunk himself and ended up, says Nilsson, on the bathroom floor "with his head resting against the toilet" (Fricke and Ressner 1988, 52).

Fricke and Ressner conclude by positioning Goldman as an "outsider" to both the sixties generation and the world of rock. Noting that he already was an adult during the sixties, they quote his early essays on rock in which he argued that it is inferior to jazz. They conclude the article with a somewhat cloying reference to Ono and Sean. Ono says that when she heard the book was coming out she phoned Sean at summer camp to warn him that it might be hurtful to him. Sean said, according to Ono, "Mommy, let's fight this one. I'll do anything. Let's fight this one" (93). The article ends as it began, with a picture of children that suggests betrayal and defiled innocence. Goldman, an outsider to both the sixties generation and the world of rock, had trespassed, and *Rolling Stone* digs in and defends its turf, its role as official voice of both. In the process, publisher Jann Wenner also defends a friend and business partner.

The primary conflict between Goldman (along with William Morrow and Company) and Yoko Ono (along with *Rolling Stone*) had both ideological and material aspects. Certainly the confontation provided splendid commercial opportunities for the conflicting parties; material motivations cannot be ignored in describing and attributing meaning to this conflict. Yet the intensity would seem to reveal tensions among beliefs that run deeper than greed. Goldman had become adept at producing his unique, and commercially attractive, kind of iconoclastic biography of a popular culture figure. His books on Lenny Bruce, Elvis Presley, and John Lennon, apart from their blatant sensationalism, did offer critiques of various social segments—the nihilism of "beat" culture; the seeming gullibility of the southern working class; and the self-important, contradictory, and often delusional tendencies of the sixties generation. Ono was a widow who had suffered the trauma of seeing her husband die violently before her eyes. She and John Lennon had publicly professed certain stances and values consistently over time, and she most probably did love John Lennon deeply. *Rolling Stone*, under Jann Wenner, had been the voice of a generation and of rock music for two decades. It took up the defense of one of rock's central heroes and of the generation that engendered and sustained the music.

LENNON AS COMMODITY

John Lennon the man was dead, but the memory and symbol of John Lennon had become both an ideological banner and a commodity. The six books, one film, and one record album about Lennon that appeared in 1988 generated over a billion dollars in gross revenues (Ferguson 1988). In addition to the *Imagine: John Lennon* package, in 1987 Yoko Ono provided unreleased interviews and audiotapes of Lennon that were put together as a year-long radio series and syndicated by Westwood One. The series began on radio stations nationwide in January 1988. (Kozinn 1988b, I:19). And the Beatles still remained big business. A 1987 compact disc release of *Sergeant Pepper* was number one on the *Billboard* charts for five weeks (Jennings 1988, 44). Youngsters who were born after the Beatles broke up were forming Beatles fan clubs. As Richard Schickel asserts about contemporary celebrities, "Death can be a career move, for careers now have a theoretically infinite life, thanks to television and video cassettes, thanks to revival houses and film festivals and the academicizing of film" (1986, 175). In addition to his symbolic importance for the sixties generation, John Lennon had attained the commercial form of eternal life that Schickel describes, so his image would remain available for many other appropriations. Still, voices in the popular press, responding to both Goldman and Ono, made sure the controversy remained philosophical as well as material.

GENERATIONAL VOICES:
EMERGING DETACHMENT

CRITIQUES OF GOLDMAN, ONO, AND LENNON

Samples from the national popular press about the battle over Lennon's memory reveal, as expected, a much less emotional, much more detached tone than the 1980 and 1981 elegies for Lennon written in the atmosphere of shared grief. Writings on the Goldman controversy reveal almost none of the intense authorial identification with the audience that characterized the elegies. The passage of time and recession of emotions resulted in a calmer, more distanced tone in the 1988 pieces on Lennon. The generation is described almost always in the third person.

This calming of passions also reflects some willingness on the part of writers, and presumably their audiences, to lessen their investment in Lennon as a generational symbol. Most writers were critical of Goldman, but they were perhaps more passionate in their attacks on Goldman than in their defenses of Lennon. They criticized Goldman for his poor research, his inflated writing style, his pandering to the prurient and sensational, and, perhaps most of all, for his meanness of spirit. Yet they often seemed to accept that much of what Goldman wrote about Lennon probably was true and that the counteroffensive by Yoko Ono and *Rolling Stone* amounted to overkill. They found themselves responding to Goldman in the context of Ono's response, a situation that perhaps leads them to be less sentimental about Lennon than they might otherwise have been.

Goldman's work is described as "malicious" (Gewen 1988, 19), "smug and nasty" (Hilburn 1988), "so relentlessly negative as to be repellent," revealing "an utter lack of charity" (Udovitch 1988, 54), and "venomous" (Harrington 1988). His writing style "employs some of the most overheated prose to be found outside a cheap romance novel" (Kakutani 1988) and is both "abstruse" and "laughable" (Lahr 1988). All the reviews of the book that I have read, with a single exception,[2] indicate that even if there is some merit in Goldman's charges, his meanness of spirit severely compromises his credibility as a biographer. He also is taken to task for his numerous factual errors, and these charges are so copious that I cannot chronicle them here. Suffice it to say the sheer volume, if not always the importance, of the errors greatly troubles the reviewers who assume that a biography, especially one that brings such serious accusations, should exhibit greater attention to detail.

Comments by reviewers also reveal the continued complex relationship of Yoko Ono with both defenders and detractors of Lennon. Several reviewers observe that Ono bears the brunt of Goldman's wrath. Waldemar Januszczak in *Guardian Weekly* (1988, 27) says "it is Yoko who gets it from both barrels." Mim Udovitch in the *Village Voice* (1988, 53) says Goldman "really can't stand" Yoko and that the second half of the book should be titled "Vilifying Yoko." Robert Hilburn, in the *Los Angeles Times* (1988, IV:9) argues that for half the book Lennon is almost a secondary character; "The real object of Goldman's ridicule and scorn is Ono." John Lahr in the *New York Times Book Review* expresses the notion most acerbically: "Obviously, Mr. Goldman feels that the wrong Lennon was shot, and he spends much of his time practicing his own crude form of character assassination." Lahr does concede, though, that "Ms. Ono is a target that is hard to miss."

Although she had defended Lennon and Ono's relationship in an article written just after Lennon's death (see 102–4, this volume), Susan Brownmiller also wrote that "the fountains of warm devotion and transferred love may not be turned on with flowering ease for Yoko Ono" (1981, 36). Although Yoko Ono did become an object of sympathy following Lennon's death, that sympathy apparently was short-lived. Robert Hilburn allowed that Ono remained a controversial figure and that some who believe she broke up the Beatles "resent her continued stewardship of the Lennon legacy" (1988, 9). It is possible that in savaging Yoko Ono as he did, Goldman could have mollified some Lennon supporters. If Lennon was a weak and selfless creature, easily led, he might have been spared much agony and indignity if he had a truly loving and supportive companion. But Goldman charges that Ono played on Lennon's insecurities in order to gain power over him and enhance her own status in the worlds of entertainment and business. A small space or seam is left for some readers sympathetic to Lennon to read Goldman's biography as an indictment of Ono more than of Lennon.

Reviewers of *The Lives of John Lennon* and *Imagine: John Lennon* were quick to point out the self-interested aspects of Ono's response to Goldman. Barry Gewen, reviewing *The Lives of John Lennon* in the *New Leader* (1988), observes that "every possible effort is being made to discredit this book" and that the campaign against the book "has a tinny ring" (18). Andrew Ferguson in the *Wall Street Journal* (1988) writes that "Ms. Ono and her son have taken the path preferred by offended celebrities: They have hit the talk shows to display their wounds." And Ferguson charges the *Rolling Stone* rebuttal to Goldman with "priggish indignation." Richard Harrington in the *Washington Post* notes that the controversy has taken on "a Rashomon-like dilemma." Do we see Lennon through "Ono's rose-colored glasses" or through Goldman's "microscope?" Harrington praises *Imagine: John Lennon* for its being revealing and evocative, yet he feels the presence of Yoko Ono all through the film and suspects Lennon himself would have preferred an honest middle ground between "Goldman's sordid iconoclasm" and "Ono and Solt's vapid protectionism" (B11).

Reviewers largely sympathetic to *Imagine: John Lennon* do not ignore Ono's presence. Michael Wilmington, in the *Los Angeles Times*, says the film at its best is a "sensitive tribute" but at its worst is a "hero-worshiping whitewash" (VI:1). Noting that the film constantly "skips away from the dark side" of Lennon's life, Wilmington suggests that "it seems less Lennon's image that is being protected here than Ono's—perhaps less through design than gratitude for her cooperation" (VI:7). Although she finds *Imagine: John Lennon* to be "a lively, entertaining film that offers a moving portrait of Lennon and his times," Janet Maslin in the *New York Times* (1988, III: 7) also notes that it is part of a public relations battle "now raging over Lennon's memory" and that it "presents a notably more sanitized and superficial portrait" of Lennon than does Goldman. Maslin says that the film, however, does what it means to—that it recaptures "much of what the Beatles meant to their contemporaries and conveys an acute and tragic sense of what was lost when Lennon died."

NEWSWEEK ON GENERATIONAL IDENTITY

Indeed, the generational theme that Maslin finds in *Imagine: John Lennon* was an important part of the 1988 discourse, though it did not dominate the discourse as it had in the wake of Lennon's death. The most comprehensive assessment of the controversy appeared in an October 17 *Newsweek* cover story titled "John Lennon: The Battle Over His Memory" (1988). The article seems less concerned with the truth of Goldman's accusations than with the effect the book might have on the sixties generation. A photospread across the first two pages of the article suggests the primary points of conflict between Goldman and the sixties generation. There are five photographs of Lennon, each with a year under it, and each revealing a different-looking Lennon. The photos suggest the chameleonlike Lennon that Goldman found while also showing a Lennon aging through phases that suggest, in the words of Andrew Solt, "The '60s and the '70s were reflected through his life to such an extent that people can't help but identify with him" (Solt and Egan 1988, 66). The photo display graphically suggests that Lennon remains an enigma and that there is truth in both versions of him.

Much of the article is devoted to a critical review of the debate between Goldman and the Ono–Wolper/Solt–*Rolling Stone* alliance. It charges that *The Lives of John Lennon* "is guaranteed to stimulate the most jaded palate" and that the "misanthropic tone" (John Lennon: The Battle . . . , 64) of the book is cause for questioning its fairness. Also, it is so rife with careless errors of fact that its overall accuracy is suspect. But *Newsweek* allows that the book has commanded attention because of "the sheer boldness of its accusations—and because it's possible some could be true" (65).

Newsweek describes the *Rolling Stone* rebuttal to Goldman as "overwrought" and goes on essentially to referee the points of contention between *Rolling Stone* and Goldman, concluding that the *Rolling Stone* investigation was hardly "intensive," as it had advertised, and that it too was guilty of factual errors and the convenient arrangement and interpretation of facts. The article also mentions the social relationship of *Rolling Stone* publisher Jann Wenner and Yoko Ono.

Newsweek states that "Yoko Ono hopes 'Imagine: John Lennon' will be the official counterdocument to the Goldman biography" (65) but concludes that the film does represent "the definitive version of the John Lennon myth" (66). This "familiar saga" of progression through the various fads and movements of the 1960s and 1970s to a point of domesticity and adulthood is now mythologized by television shows such as "Family Ties" and "thirtysomething." Lennon and the baby boom generation, says *Newsweek*, are wedded in this saga. *Newsweek* quotes a visitor who came from Atlanta to New York to celebrate Lennon's birthday: "It seems like everything he got into, I got into at about the same time." (67). This indelible wedding of Lennon and a generation is "the myth Yoko Ono wants graven in stone and handed down to posterity. And it's the myth Goldman had blasphemed" (67).

The battle is over a generation's view of its history. The stakes are high because "if Lennon was a fraud, where does that leave the values he was thought to embody?" (67). *Newsweek* zeros in on the crucial identity aspects of the controversy, as members of the sixties generation hang on precariously to some sense of identity rooted in sixties communitas, in a sense of collective sharing of values such as honesty and openness and a corresponding disdain for social artifice and "phoniness."

Newsweek makes the point well by considering why so many Lennon defenders should be upset at Goldman's charges that Lennon committed homosexual acts and may have been bisexual. Why should it matter "that Lennon was doing stuff they don't think is wrong in the first place?" (68). The issue, *Newsweek* argues, is that it would reveal Lennon as a fraud, and it would be deeply worrisome since "belief in John's unflinching honesty is one of the prime articles of faith among the Lennon Left" (68).

The article devotes a full column to Goldman's charges that he is bucking a rock establishment with a vested interest in icons such as Lennon and Presley. Goldman says "as long as I talked the rock-and-roll party line I was OK with *Rolling Stone*" (73). Goldman argues that the real issue is the kind of life that pop stars lead—"the life of Caesar, and we all know where the life of Caesar leads" (73). Goldman believes he is the recipient of attacks, based on blind adherence to an ideology, the very kind that used to infuriate the sixties counterculture.

Newsweek quotes rock critic Dave Marsh, who says that Goldman and Ono "should both give it a rest. . . . They are falsifying history on both sides. The truth is in the music. You want the truth, go listen" (73). *Newsweek* seems comfortable with this assessment, noting that Lennon and the Beatles keep attracting a sizable audience out of each new generation of music listeners. The article quotes seventeen-year-olds who find joy and meaning in that music today, though they bend it to their needs. A youngster says Lennon's 1968 song "Revolution" is a "real teenage song" (73). The song was, in 1968 of course, an important part of the dialogue in an internal rift in the counterculture and New Left over the use of violent means of protest.

Newsweek doubts that Goldman really can do much damage, for sixties heroes like Lennon and John F. Kennedy "could teach Ronald Reagan a thing or two about Teflon images. . . . Except to the relatively few people who actually had to deal with the man himself, an image is all that ever mattered anyway. That and the music" (73).

A SYMBOLIC NARROWING OF LENNON

Although *Newsweek* suggests Lennon's image may outlast Goldman's attempt to tarnish it, other writers fear that Lennon's image may never be the same after Goldman. Caught between Goldman's attack and

Ono's sanitizing, two long pieces on Goldman and Lennon seek a middle ground and suggest that the sixties generation was in retreat from sustained attacks and its own self-doubts. Luc Sante in the *New York Review of Books* and Louis Menand in the *New Republic* both roundly criticize Goldman, but they offer defenses of, and tributes to, Lennon that narrow his symbolic scope considerably. Both writers appear to accept that Lennon's supposed "househusband phase" was probably less than Lennon and Ono made it out to be, and neither deals with Lennon as a symbol of transition to adulthood or as a symbol of communitas. Instead, they locate Lennon's significance back in the era of the youth culture. He and the generation had grandiose dreams that exceeded their grasp. Lennon's legacy lies in his wit and in how he articulated the moods and feelings of youth, they seem to argue. In view of Goldman's book, seven years of sixties bashing, and seven more years of life experience for the sixties generation, Sante and Menand seek to lighten the symbolic load on John Lennon and portray him as an articulator of the single most distinctive aspect of the sixties generation—its indelible identification with the feelings of youth. Both imply that this legacy is not necessarily bad.

In a long essay in the *New York Review of Books* covering several works on Lennon and the Beatles titled "Beatlephobia," Luc Sante's critique of Goldman is the most comprehensive and careful (1988). Sante mentions that Joyce Carol Oates termed Goldman's and several other biographies of that year "pathography" (1988, 46), but suggests that Goldman's work is so bitter and cynical that it "almost deserves a category all its own" (31). Sante carefully describes seven of Goldman's "techniques of defamation" (for example, "The Indelible Anecdote," "The Gratuitous Slur," "Guilt by Association"). Sante says that, aside from the pure venality of the writer and publisher, the book exists because Lennon and the Beatles "somehow became symbolic representations of an entire generation" (34).

The new wave of material on Lennon and the Beatles, then, really is "about the Sixties" and the extraordinary impact the Beatles had on that time. The problem, Sante says, is that it is difficult to measure the Beatles' influence because the sixties are a "time being both too far away and not far enough" (30). We can speculate, but not explain, why the Beatles were so influential, something quite different from merely being popular. What cannot be adequately explained, Sante proposes, is easily transformed into legend. In this suggestion, Sante seems to discount the experience of communitas. The 1988 crop of books on Lennon and the Beatles "is mostly the product of seeds planted in the wake of Lennon's killing" (30). Lennon is the focus of this historical and generational dialogue because he was the only Beatle "to harbor the appropriate messianic ambitions" and because he was "the most complex and most vulnerable" among them.

That Goldman had to resort to so many different strategies to attack him, testifies to the complexity of his character. Sante notes the contradictory nature of Lennon and Ono's famous "bed-in" for peace: "The Lennon–Ono program and its mystique are pretty well summed up by this stunt, which was at once presumptious, well-meaning, self-important, irrelevant, humorous, embarrassing, lax, wan, dopey, and oddly sweet" (35). Sante notes that the song "Imagine," which has become "the theme song of his posthumous devotion," is rife with contradictions. It, too, is simultaneously presumptuous and well-meaning, and Sante says Lennon seemed unaware of the contradictions of filming a video of his performing the song and singing the words "Imagine no possessions" while dressed in a white suit in a white room in a mansion (35).

Lennon most clearly mirrored the generation that adores him in these contradictions. Both Lennon and the sixties generation harbored vast ambitions that became their undoing. Lennon, says Sante, was best at being a "provocateur and mischief-maker" (35). The best "work" of the sixties generation, too, Sante suggests, was its theatrical flamboyance and street theater, its ability to dramatize its concerns. When it took itself seriously as a counterculture, it overreached and soon evaporated into airy idealism. After Lennon's death, Sante remembers the moment that best conveyed what had died: During a Beatles press conference when they arrived in New York in 1964, Lennon was asked by a reporter, "How did you find America?" He replied, "We turned left at Greenland" (35). Lennon's legacy, and perhaps the legacy of the sixties generation, is a youthful cheekiness at once charming and biting, both endearing and oppositional. Lennon and the sixties represent, for Sante, more a style than an ideology.

The notion of Lennon as a representative of something peculiarly youthful is developed also in a review essay in the *New Republic* by Louis Menand (1988). Before considering Lennon's symbolic value for his generation, Menand does offer one straightforward explanation for the Beatles' and John Lennon's tremendous influence. The Beatles were adored by the press. Their combination of wit, intuition, and self-deprecation appealed to a press unaccustomed to such things from pop music stars. The middle class found the Beatles' insouciance enchanting perhaps because it appeared not as class antagonism but as the brashness of youth. Menand says Lennon was "to a significant degree the Beatles' public voice" (32) and that Lennon in his post-Beatle days cultivated the alternative press (which would become in large part the rock establishment by the time of his death). He was much more accessible than the other Beatles or other superstars like Bob Dylan or Mick Jagger. The payoff, Menand says, is that the press responded by honoring the image of the Lennons as the prototype of the counterculture marriage and by defending them (32).

According to Menand, Lennon and the Beatles were important to the sixties generation largely because their sound was not the sound of responsible adulthood. Menand says the youth culture begins essentially with *Catcher in the Rye*—"a book whose hero is an almost pathological hater of adulthood." The youth culture exhibited a hostility to growing up, and its music, sixties rock, was about dropping out for middle-class students. Menand posits that the ordinary adolescent resistance to growing up "became generalized into the culture at large in the 60's" (35). Observing that society was so overrun with the young that it could tolerate dropouts, Menand says, "this seems one of those rare instances when the baby boom, which is supposed to explain everything about postwar American life, actually does explain something" (35).

Lennon and the Beatles, according to Menand, "acted out the positive side of this not growing up" (35). Though most of the sixties generation have grown past that adolescent mode of experiencing, they are deeply imbued with it, and Lennon and the sixties are remembered today because "it still seems important for adults well past 30 to remind themselves occasionally of the thrill they once felt when, in the exuberance of being 'youth' they scorned the trappings of adulthood" (35). Menand says it is Lennon more than any other figure from the period who provides these moments. Lennon's voice and image seem always "so bracingly indifferent to convention," and his style "makes you want to let your own light shine a little too. There is nothing complicated about what he expressed. It's just a kind of tonic, sometimes still a necessary one" (35). Menand suggests that in 1988, Lennon has taken on a more personal meaning, as a symbol of the period of youth that is more likely to be experienced privately. The youth culture closed, he argues, with Lennon's death.

Both Sante and Menand propose that 1988 reveals a less collective and emotional appropriation of Lennon; Lennon is important, says Sante, because he mirrors the contradictions of a generation, and ultimately shows how they share in the same kinds of limitations. Menand sees the primary legacy of the sixties generation as the mood of swaggering youth, and Lennon's image and music still articulate the vital but undirected energy of youth. Both writers point to directions the post-Goldman generational view of Lennon might take. And both suggest that the generation's sense of identity and its situation in the social order will be aided by less grandiose visions of its past and John Lennon. Yet, neither writer repudiates the past or the generation's identity rooted in the feelings of youth. As Menand says, "It's just a kind of tonic." And it may be the distinctive gift that the generation can bring to the social order.

In their 1989 longitudinal study of sixties activists, Jack Whalen and Richard Flacks (2) argue that the redefining of adulthood was probably the single theme that united the sixties youth revolt. The youth culture rejected the notion of an adulthood bound by sets of roles and relationships, and in seeking the freedom to reform identity continuously, the sixties generation did indeed reject established notions of adulthood. The feeling of being young is one aspect of their past they seem to carry with them throughout their lives, and they may be in the process of redefining adulthood.

LENNON, EVANGELISM, AND DAMNATION

The complexity of reintegration is evident in an essay by Harold Smith in *Christianity Today* (1988). Smith suggests the controversy over Goldman's biography of John Lennon reveals that the sixties generation has its identity so shaken that it stands ready to accept Christianity and that the evangelical Christian church should welcome this confused segment. Smith's invitation to let go of old antagonisms seems both reintegrative and co-opting. Is there really a place for the voices and unique experiences of sixties people in the evangelical church? Or is the generation simply so beaten down that it is ripe for conversion? That is, will accepting this new group alter the meaning system of the church or will it require the new group's acceptance of the existing meaning system? Smith leaves these questions unanswered.

Smith indicates some identification with the sixties generation and defines the crisis over John Lennon thusly:

Lennon was, perhaps the last, best hope for a now middle-aged generation wanting the assurance that it did not demonstrate in vain; that its youthful idealisms really do have a place in the real world—venereal disease and drug addiction notwithstanding. A fallen hero, a martyr, Lennon died—or so the public perception goes—with his idealism intact, his vision for peace in focus. Now we are told that his life was programmed to self-destruct. (14)

Common sense, Smith reminds, tells us it could be no other way, for Lennon did live out the conseqences of a self-indulgent ideology. The important point about this controversy, says Smith, is not the defense or debunking of Lennon and the sixties but that a "darker reality" underlies the conflict. That is that the sixties generation suffers a nagging sense of hopelessness, in stark contrast to its memories of its energy, bright spirit, and endless hopes.

Smith says the present seems bleak to sixties people because the gods of the sixties were uncontrollable and destructive. A gospel built on hedonism and a hazy concept of "luv" has degenerated into alienation and self-centeredness. Smith indicates the importance of considering the consequences over the next thirty to forty years of the, by-now chronic, alienation of the largest single generation ever to populate the United States. Smith suggests that the church can step into this breach, that it "has a mission field cut out for it that twenty years ago it was unwilling to acknowledge" (15). Smith says the church in effect "took sides" during the conflicts of the sixties; it should have been a "community of hurting and healed people": instead it "polarized around sociopolitical issues and became a closed community" (15).

The church may have another chance at this generation, he argues, because the recent events over Lennon reveal them to be struggling for a vision that can be trusted. Ironically, they experience hopelessness *because* of their latent idealism. Smith proposes that having their own children will increase the potential for spiritual renewal among this generation, since it is not likely to want its own children "to wander from acid to ashram to whatever is next in search of truth" (15).

Concluding that the "halcyon days of the sixties were short-lived and short-sighted," Smith sees little point in mourning their passing or wallowing in despair at the lost ideals of the period. The church is now in a position to provide a way out of that past: "Burned by sensuality, hedonism, and materialism, the sixties generation is now primed to give true peace a chance" (15). This entry of a voice of established religion into the generational dialogue may have signaled a true reintegrative move on the part of an established institution—a move made possible by the weakened individual and collective identities of members of the sixties generation that render them ripe for co-optation or absorption.

There are obvious reasons for the success of Goldman's biography. A mass-mediated celebrity society thrives on gossip and debunking, which perform an old carnivalesque function of bringing down those high in the social order. Also, Goldman had an established track record with this kind of "pathography," and a major publisher was willing to promote it. But a work as deeply cruel as Goldman's can find purchase only in a culture already receptive to such impulses. The book's success and the ensuing controversy had much to do with the broader context of a scapegoating of the sixties in the conservative revolution of the 1980s.

Though critics used terms such as "small," "mean," or "misanthropic" to describe Goldman's work, the book expresses, at heart, a tone of retributive damnation. In the desecration of Lennon, a generation and the weaknesses of liberalism that engendered it are damned almost beyond redemption. Lennon's final days are spent in darkness and evil, and that, suggests the tale, is the proper end of a generation and a libertine philosophy that is seen as having sapped a nation's strength and weakened its moral fiber. In the almost religious fervor of the conservative swing of the United States in the 1980s, the "permissiveness" that characterized the sixties may be seen as a snake in the garden that must suffer expulsion and damnation. Attacks on permissiveness; the sanctification of the nuclear family; calls for more authoritarian approaches to education; and strident sexism, racism, and homophopia are practical political issues and signals of an ideological conflict over interpretations of history, especially the crucial period of the sixties (Sayres, Stephanson, Aronowitz, and Jameson 1984, 8).

The discrediting of "liberalism" and "permissiveness" has been a major component of public discourse in the Reagan–Bush Era; witness the 1988 and 1992 presidential campaigns, and the 1990 debate over a constitutional amendment to ban desecration of the American flag. At a press conference in Salt Lake City in early 1983, long-time Reagan aide Lyn Nofziger was asked how he would run a Reagan campaign if Walter Mondale were the Democratic nominee in 1984. Nofziger said the first strategy that came to mind would be to ignore Mondale and run against Jimmy Carter or, he reflected, Ted Kennedy. It may be safely generalized that Republican strategy at the national level in the 1980s was to run generally against liberalism and the Democrats' association with that supposedly failed philosophy. Indeed, liberalism became so discredited that it come to be called by 1988, only partly in jest, the "L word," as if it were an obscenity.

The relationship of the sixties generation to this state of affairs is as follows. By conservative reasoning America was weakened and fragmented in the 1960s and early 1970s, largely by youth and race segments. The disorder of the times was the fault of "permissive" liberals in power (from presidents to school principals) who acquiesced to these groups on both domestic and foreign policy issues (Ehrenreich 1989; Matusow 1984). On the political front, the word "liberal" was becoming a term of opprobrium, and on the cultural front the sixties nirvana of sex, drugs, and rock and roll became an eighties hell of AIDS, crack cocaine, and dissolute frauds like John Lennon—thus the tone of damnation in Goldman, who relentlessly pursues Lennon into every dark corner of his existence and finally demands nothing but total surrender.

The crisis for members of the sixties generation was not necessarily that history had seemed to discredit much of their libertine philosophy—that much was obvious—but the attack on them exacerbated their self-doubts as expressed in the grieving for Lennon and, worse, seemed possibly to stand in the way of their efforts to reintegrate. It is almost as if the eighties saw a reigniting of the crisis phase of contemporary social drama, with forces against the sixties threatening much of the generation's identity base.

NOTE

1. In the late 1970s the Lennons purchased about 250 purebred Holstein cows and kept them on land they owned near the Catskills. In 1980 one of the cows sold for $265,000 at the New York State Fair. One of the Lennon farm managers told Laurence Shames, "That Yoko writes up a mean pedigree. She's the one who really knows the business, ya know" (Shames 1980, 31–38.

2. Of more than thirty magazine and newspaper articles on this controversy that I collected from personal files and from the *Reader's Guide* and *Los Angeles Times*, *Washington Post*, and *New York Times* indexes, only one accepted Goldman's argument without reservation. Paul Gray, in *Time*, writes that "Goldman deserves considerable credit for making such sordid, depressing material compulsively readable. *The Lives of John Lennon* is a far more balanced and objective biography than his *Elvis* (1981)" (1988, 77).

8

The Sixties Generation in the 1980s

The Goldman controversy was part of a cultural/political process in the 1980s that pushed the sixties generation out of its self-absorbed identity crisis of 1980 and back into the arena of social conflict. In this development we see more clearly the development of social drama, as this segment turns more to considerations of its relation to the social whole. Some of the generational responses to conservative attacks on the sixties show that various writers assuming they speak for the sixties generation do so in conciliatory tones, offering compromise. However, they refuse to surrender their sense of identity and allow conservative critics to define them and the social order. The battle over the "meaning" of the sixties is an example of deep divisions over meaning that characterize social drama. The present state of conflict and division suggests the inability of present symbols and meaning systems to describe and organize the experience for most of society and that new symbols for a reintegrated social order are not yet in evidence.

The conflicts between conservative critics and the sixties generation occurred in a crowded and complex battlefield. James Carey, correctly I think, identifies race and gender as the two most significant emergent identity forms of the past twenty years. The sixties generation segment that is the focus of this study has conflicted relations with both of these identity forms, which themselves have been under attack by conservatives in the 1980s.

In the sixties, "blacks" emerged as a new historical subject. In the new vocabulary, "Afro-American became the sign of militant identity, a statement of cultural autonomy and international racial solidarity with Africa" (Sayres, Stephanson, Aronowitz, and Jameson 1984, 4). New "black" identity involved a shift away from reliance on white, liberal

143

paternalism. The first significant rift between militant black leaders and conventional liberals occurred as early as the 1964 Democratic National Convention (Gitlin 1987, 152–62). The break between black and white sixties radicals was complete by 1968 when the Student Nonviolent Coordinating Committee (SNCC) forced out all of its white staff members (168). At the other end of the sixties generation spectrum, relations were no better. Blacks looked on the hippie culture with disdain and derision. Noting that there probably were fewer than fifty black hippies in San Francisco's Haight-Ashbury district, Nicholas von Hoffman found that blacks could not empathize with white, middle-class kids who reject the very material things blacks want. Blacks, says von Hoffman (1968, 125), see hippies as an affront:

> So rich, so precious, so secure, so much to the manner [*sic*] born, they can despise the money, the cleanliness, the comfort, the balanced diet, the vitamins, and the living room carpets black people have been willing to die for.

Von Hoffman relates a confrontation between hippies and a black activist in the Fillmore district. The black sneers at the hippies, "I don't want you to love me. . . . You better go get your hair cut, get a job, and teach your people to defend themselves" (127). In the contracting economy of the 1970s and early 1980s, many of the white, middle-class sixties generation found themselves consciously or unconsciously in conflict with blacks and other racial and ethnic minorities over jobs or professional school admissions as a result of civil rights legislation that the sixties people had themselves supported. Although members of the sixties generation and baby boomers in general indicate fewer racist tendencies on surveys than do older and younger segments, the libertarian impulses of many of them may well reflect submerged racial feelings in reaction to ideological and perceived material conflicts with blacks (Whalen and Flack 1989, 231–33).

Intragenerational conflict over gender is even more complex than conflict over racial identity. I have discussed in Chapter 6 how questions of gender and sexual equality surfaced in elegies for John Lennon. Some writers portrayed Lennon and Ono's marriage as a model for gender equality, and others quoted Lennon and Ono on sexism in the counterculture. Women certainly have problems accepting central symbols of sixties communitas such as sex, drugs, and rock and roll, which reflect primarily male desires and modes of behavior. Women of the sixties generation generally are less prone to nostalgia for the sixties than men. Observing that many radical feminists came out of the sixties left and counterculture, Ellen Willis argues (1989, 171) that one legacy of that era for women is "pent-up rage at men's one-sided exploitative view of sexual freedom" that characterized the so-called "sexual revolution" of the sixties. That period and the anger it engendered have left unresolved conflict about sexuality, according to Willis. This rage crosses racial lines, too; Todd Gitlin notes (1987, 169) that in 1968 Stokely Carmichael ridiculed demands for sexual equality made by female members of Student Nonviolent Coordinating Committee.

Desires for racial, sexual, cultural, and political equality were conflicted and contradictory in the sixties and remain so in the present. Conservatives attribute their catalog of present-day evils such as promiscuity, illicit drug use, abortion, racial violence, rising crime rates, and the breakdown of the nuclear family to a single radical impulse named "the sixties." Thus, whether intentionally or not, conservative social critics exploit divisions among sixties people, and sixties people, who once might have shared a vision of equality and freedom, now divide along lines of race and gender that often render them as far from each other as they are from older conservatives.

An interesting example of such fragmenting is the case of heavy metal rock music. Heavy metal came under siege in the 1980s from both the right wing and the rock establishment, thus suggesting a complex generational conflict involving the older right wing, the early baby boomers, and the younger fans who were very much within the tradition of sixties counterculture values of hedonism and "authenticity." Deena Weinstein, in *Heavy Metal: A Cultural Sociology* (1991), argues convincingly that heavy metal was probably the clearest and purest remaining form of sixties acid rock. But its working-class image and apolitical, diffuse energy troubled rock purists and the rock criticism establishment. Critics from the religious right wing took its satanic symbols and seemingly nihilistic lyrics quite literally. Weinstein offers a compelling account of the exegetical free-for-all engendered by the Senate record-labeling hearings in September 1985. Did Ozzy Osbourne's "Suicide Solution" mean that he advocated suicide or that he was writing about alchohol as a liquid (solution) that slowly kills? Weinstein describes several such points of analysis which most often eluded the committee questioners

SIXTIES UNDER SIEGE

In his study of the demise of liberalism, Allen Matusow observed, "In 1968 Ronald Reagan had been too conservative for the Republican Party. In 1980, running on a platform to repeal the cultural as well as the political legacy of the sixties, he easily won the presidency of the United States" (1984, 439). By the end of Reagan's second term in 1988, many in the sixties generation felt their defining era and values to be under siege. The *Newsweek* story on the Lennon controversy alludes to this feeling ("John Lennon: The Battle . . . ," 73), noting that many in the rock establishment saw Goldman's book as part of a larger effort in the 1980s to discredit the sixties.

Rock and roll was the only unsullied cultural marker left—sex and drugs had been so tainted by AIDS and crack cocaine—so Goldman's book seemed a particularly pointed assault. *Newsweek* described the feelings of many sixties people: The "anti-rock right" is trying to "shrivel the utopian expansiveness expressed in songs like Lennon's 'Imagine'" (73). The same article describes Allan Bloom's "improbable bestseller," *The Closing of the American Mind* (1987), as "a brief for cultural conservatism whose rockophobic fulminations read like a slightly more elegant version of Goldman" (73).

Bloom's book generated wide-ranging responses that crossed many segmental lines in American society. Bloom specifically singled out the sixties as the period when American universities lost their way and gave up on what Bloom believes to be their primary mission—the direct transmission of a Western cultural heritage and a corresponding set of values. The primary villains, in his analysis, are "liberal" faculty and administrators during that period who subscribed to a relativistic philosophy and subsequently acquiesced to pressures from student rebels and instituted so-called reforms that have gutted our higher education system. Bloom was on the faculty at Cornell in 1969 when militant black students bearing arms took over several university buildings. The sixties generation as a whole is criticized by implication in Bloom's strident assessment of the effects of rock music. Bloom equates rock music experientially with drug addiction and believes its mere existence signals the end of civilization, which he suggests may be symbolized in the image of a thirteen-year-old boy sitting in his living room doing homework while watching MTV:

A pubescent child whose body throbs with orgasmic rhythms; whose feelings are made articulate in hymns to the joys of onanism or the killing of parents; whose ambition is to win fame and wealth in imitating the drag-queen who makes the music. In short, life is made into a non-stop, commercially prepackaged masturbational fantasy. (1987, 75)

Bloom's attack on rock music and Goldman's attack on John Lennon can be read as part of a larger conservative cultural attempt to blame permissive liberalism for social disorder in the sixties. The sixties generation and its values (or lack thereof) is criticized, both explicitly and implicity, as the rotten fruit of that liberalism.

GENERATIONAL RESPONSES TO ALLAN BLOOM

In a long review in the *Voice Literary Supplement* (1989), Maria Margaronis discusses Bloom's book, E. D. Hirsch's *Cultural Literacy: What Every American Needs to Know,* and William Bennett's *Our Children and Our Country: Improving America's Schools and Affirming the Common Culture.* Asserting that these are among a number of books in other fields in the 1980s that "set public discussion firmly on conservative ground," Margaronis says their "lingo crops up" throughout the national discourse. She finds it in op-ed pieces in major newspapers, in network television specials about America's ignorant youth, in George's Bush's partisan barbs that "value-free education" has caused a national drug problem, and in "the orgy of handwringing that greeted Stanford University's decision to broaden its core curriculum" (1989, 12).

The work of these "cultural warriors" of the Reagan years, says Margaronis, is part of "the right's bid to take back the culture from the children of the 60's" (12). Calls for "excellence in education" all too easily mask a more authoritarian agenda of "school prayer (to God or the flag), an end to sex education, 'moral literacy,' and obeisance to Western Civilization" (12). Margaronis suggests that Bloom was useful to the right because he kept the public discussion in a lofty, realm away from the material world. Ironically, the multipronged attack reveals that the conservatives themselves know our culture is pluralistic; thus we get "Bloom for the highbrows, Bennett for the hardcore, Hirsch for the practical, [Lynn] Cheney for those who love art" (13).

Margaronis's critique allows that at an ideal level, the right's crusade for a common language and common culture are fundamentally reintegrative; she does note the progressive elements in Hirsch's belief that cultural literacy provides a path of opportunity for disadvantaged children. But Margaronis argues that the right is trying to "invent a national culture," amid understandable uncertainties about the question of "what, after all binds the country together?" (15). She notes that our pluralism and cultural diversity are simply too great for the success of such an agenda. Her argument also illustrates aspects of the redressive phase of social drama. As one group assumes political dominance it attempts to redefine public discourse and proposes a forced kind of reintegration that returns to the past and attempts to re-create the social order before the breach. The theory of social drama posits that such an act is impossible, that the eruption of social drama always will alter the social order. If there is reintegration, it will take place under new terms and symbols.

In an interview in *New Perspectives Quarterly*, California state legislator and former sixties activist Tom Hayden directly contradicts some of Bloom's assertions about the sixties (1988, 20–25). Hayden's responses reveal the contested nature of meaning that characterizes much present-day public discourse, for Hayden claims that various examples Bloom uses to make points critical of sixties rebels prove the opposite of what he intends. Hayden allows that Bloom is correct that our campuses are morally deficient, that they are too specialized, and that objectivity masks as moral neutralism. Hayden, however, attributes these problems to totally different causes. Noting Bloom's comparison of armed black activists to Nazi storm troopers, Hayden argues that the universities were conducting weapons research and that professors were architects of the Vietnam war. It was they who were asking students to keep quiet and be "good Germans." Protesting students, argues Hayden, were "the exact opposite of Nazi storm troopers" (20).

As for moral relativism, Hayden asserts that sixties activists confronted an amoral society and materialistic universities. Hayden charges Bloom with contradicting himself by arguing that universities have been ruined by student demands for "relevance." He points out that Bloom conveniently forgets universities always have been "relevant" to the military industrial complex, to agribusiness, and to the nuclear arms race. Bloom's charges should fall, says Hayden, with equal force on those he protects: "Speaking of mindlessness, how should we regard the official claim that the US was in Viet Nam to stop Chinese communism: Speaking of moral relativism, how are we to interpret Edward Teller's views on limited nuclear war?" (1988, 22). Making reference to the context of sixties bashing, Hayden says Bloom should remember that the sixties are over; in the present context of scapegoating, "Bloom is still trying to metaphorically annihilate this pathetic handful of blacks with their shotguns" (23). Several observers have suggested that, at heart, Bloom's book was a reaction to being "traumatized" by the armed black activists at Cornell (Atlas 1988; Bruning 1987; Greider 1987, 40).

Other writers challenged Bloom's assault on the sixties generation. Ellen Goodman, in her nationally syndicated column (1987) accused Bloom of "sixties bashing" and sugggested that his book is appropriate for an age in which citizens are being seen as consumers. The book, she charges, is basically a guide for "consumers" of college education.

Veteran rock critic Robert Hilburn (1987) seems puzzled by Bloom's focus on rock music and adolescence. He suspects Bloom probably does not know about "inspiring, high-principled artists" (III:66) such as Bob Dylan, the Beatles, Van Morrison, Bruce Springsteen, and U2. Bloom, charges Hilburn, also seems unaware that rock and the sixties generation grew together and that "the artistic pulse of the music now reaches a demographic that is creeping past 50" (III:66).

Two critics also pointed out an ominous preaching tone in Bloom. David Gates in *Newsweek* (1987) categorizes Bloom's work as part of "an earnest but confused back-to-basics trend" (72) and suggests also that "Bloom sounds as if he's warming up for a guest shot on the 700 Club, calling for a return to moral certainty—at least as a philosophical point of departure—and spattering on about the evils of rock and roll" (73). Willian Greider in *Rolling Stone* (1987) asks, after listing Bloom's numerous indictments of modern society and popular culture, if we have not heard this all before:

> Doesn't Bloom sound an awful lot like Jerry Falwell and the other right-wing televangelists? Running down Bloom's diagnosis of our social ills, I realized it is a perfect fit with the standard born-again sermon, covering the same ground from the Good Book to rock & roll. Maybe this, too, explains Bloom's popularity—he is peddling fundamentalism for highbrows." (40)

In a *National Review* article (1988), William Tucker underscores the religious motif in conservative critiques of the sixties. Observing the twentieth reunion of activists from Columbia University with requisite skepticism, Tucker concludes, "What I was looking for at Columbia, I suppose, and never really did find, was some small sign of *penitence* [italics mine]" (38).

Writers speaking to and for the sixties generation sensed a kind of religious fervor in the fulminations of Bloom and Goldman and others and seemed very much aware they had been under a cultural attack for some time. Despite the specific counters to Bloom and criticisms of his work and the agenda perceived to be behind it, some sixties voices responded to the perception of attack in surprisingly conciliatory tones. Prominent pieces in the popular press in the late 1980s reveal the sixties generation in retreat to some extent.

DEFENSE AND DEFENSIVENESS

The most comprehensive expression of this sense of retreat can be seen in the September 5, 1988, edition of *Newsweek*, which appeared about six weeks before the cover story issue on the John Lennon controversy. The September 5 stories were partly a response to generational issues raised in the presidential campaign. In back-to-back essays titled "Decade Shock" and "The Sixties Complex" Tom Morganthau and Tom Mathews react to a perceived context of continued generational warfare.

Morganthau notes the irony that the selection of Dan Quayle as George Bush's running mate has sparked a reexamination of the sixties, for, in Morganthau's words, "Dan Quayle glided into manhood as if the 1960s had never happened—and that, for George Bush and the Republican Party, may be precisely the point" (1988, 14). Yet Quayle's National Guard service has called up questions of his avoiding regular service which would have exposed him to combat duty in Vietnam. Present events reveal, says Morganthau, that "like the baby-boom generation itself, memories of the decade form an undigested lump in the national experience" (14).

Morganthau offers an assessment of the sixties from the point of view of the sixties generation, trying to be fair about its accomplishments and shortcomings. He begins by admitting that a generation's grand dreams and ideals largely have gone unfulfilled. The lesson, he reminds, is that things tend to remain the same. A generation "intoxicated by the bubble of limitless possibility—unparalleled affluence, unrestricted hedonism, the dawn of a new age in human relations—now finds itself encumbered by the same gravitational laws that confined its elders" (15). What Morganthau offers as an olive branch is a tempered repudiation of sixties ideals and a humbling admission that the generation did not change the world. But he goes on to note that the most significant achievement of the decade was the civil rights revolution, and he mentions Martin Luther King.

Oddly, the sixties movement Morganthau praises is the one that owed little to the mainstream of the white, middle-class sixties generation. Morganthau cites Vietnam as the reason for the main political legacies of the sixties: first, that America is not invincible and, second, that "political leaders cannot be trusted" (15). Morganthau does not pull punches on Vietnam, calling it "the wrong war at the wrong time in the wrong place" (15). He allows, though, that one negative legacy is a kind of knee-jerk nonintervention policy that can lead to sinister undercover exploits. The military draft, a fact of life for every male baby boomer, was, Morganthau says, mostly responsible for the power of the antiwar movement on college campuses. Morganthau admits that the draft revealed deep class divisions in American society and that its unfairness "is one of the least noble aspects of America's involvement in Vietnam" (16). Morganthau also suggests—incorrectly as it turned out—that Dan Quayle's use of a middle-class loophole in joinging the reserves "may yet hurt Bush with blue-collar voters" (16).

Perhaps as a way of validating his final plea, Morganthau argues that the one lasting and worthwhile cultural legacy of the 1960s was its affirmation of tolerance: "Even in the conservative 1980s, it is OK to be black, OK to be female, OK to be Christian or Jew—which is no small gain for the nation and its increasingly diverse population" (16). Morganthau concludes by asking whether tolerance may be extended to "the survivors of the '60s as well . . . repentant or not" (16), and he goes on to note what seems to have been a generation-based cultural persecution of Supreme Court nominee Douglas Ginsburg for his essentially generational transgression of smoking marijuana. Quayle, Morganthau notes, seems to be getting the benefit of the doubt regarding his National Guard service. Morganthau's voice suggests that many members of a once-defiant antistructure counterculture even now may not always have a choice in assuming leadership roles in the social structure.

Tom Mathews, in the next essay, observes that "right now we're settling old scores and revisiting the sins of a decade. It's time for an amnesty" (1988, 17). Mathews notes the media saturation of sixties stories and argues that apart from mere nostalgia many of them involve "visiting the sins of a decade on those who grew up and out of it" (17). Referring to a kind of cultural and generational persecution of Douglas Ginsburg, Gary Hart, and even Dan Quayle, Mathews also uses religious terms to describe the situation, saying that all of the above "have stepped forward to confess and be saved" (17). He suggests his generation is being put through a national exercise in mortification "by way of the Great Cultural Prosecution that has fallen upon us today" (18). Only half humorously, Mathews posits that "model prisoners will need model confessions. Here is mine" (18).

Mathews admits he avoided Vietnam by creating a daughter "a little prematurely" and by enrolling in graduate school, thus qualifying for a "double-dip" draft deferment. He allows, of course, that like many others of his generation, he was not as idealistic as sixties myth suggests. About drugs, Mathews is less clear. He used marijuana. But as for what he and his generation should tell today's kids, he suggests using the example of Woodstock to tell a direct and simple truth about drugs: "Woodstock did demonstrate that if you do enough dope you can put up with anything for three days" (20). The moral suggested is that just putting up with things should not really be the point of life.

About generational warfare on the campuses, Mathews confesses that he genuinely liked an old conservative professor at Columbia University and that in the midst of the student revolts the professor performed an act of consideration and kindness that caused Mathews to question the stridency of the student movement and the appropriateness of its targets.

Having shown some penitence, Mathews concludes by asking if we cannot call for a truce over the sixties; asks if his generation can be given a full pardon, intimating perhaps that his generation deserves at least what Richard Nixon got. Both essays respond to eight years of sixties bashing that sometimes reached an evangelical pitch, and both, though sometimes playful in tone, offer supplication and call for a truce. These essays appeared at just about the time Albert Goldman's biography of John Lennon was arriving in bookstores.

As revealed in the Mathews and Morganthau essays, the sixties generation was very much on the defensive on the issue of drugs by the late 1980s. The situation seemed to be that newer and stronger drugs—crack cocaine, newly developed strains of marijuana, and the hallucinogenic PCP—made drug use more dangerous and more of a social problem. But the situation in the late 1980s had also to do with a feature of social drama: that meaning systems change over its course. Drug use in the 1980s occurred in a significantly different cultural context than that which existed for the sixties generation. Todd Gitlin argues that seventies and eighties youth have taken drug use for granted, but "do not associate it with spirituality or hunger for transcendence" (1989, 354). For many of the sixties generation, drug use, mostly marijuana and to a lesser extent LSD, was charged with political and cultural significance. It was a way of identifying with a group and of entering the liminoid arena of communitas. Drug use occurred within a prescribed meaning system and often was a significant means of identification. Carey suggests that "identity coordinates" shift during times of social dislocation. In the sixties many took on one identity coordinate of *head,* a term that meant much more than "drug user." It identified one with certain drugs and with an emerging youth counterculture.

Tom Mathews is ambivalent about his generation's drug use. Being true to his own experience and presumably speaking for many of his cohort, Mathews does not preach that drugs were bad. Rather, he suggests that they do not do much good. He is willing to recant counterculture enthusiasm for the usefulness of mind-expanding drugs, but he will not deliver a jeremiad on their evil effects.

In a *Time* magazine essay (1989, 104) focusing on the dilemmas sixties people now face regarding their previous drug use, Walter Shapiro offers conditional penitence for himself and his generation. Shapiro opens with a fairly standard sixties generation response to its drug-use history—he simply outgrew it. Giving up marijuana in the mid-1970s, says Shapiro, "was not a wrenching moral decision, but rather an aesthetic rite of passage as my palate began to savor California Chardonnay." Shapiro generalizes here the experience of his generation, that drug use was associated with youth and with a particularly intense period of a youth culture that has moved into the mainstream and now appreciates what other segments would agree are the finer things in life. The statement is ingratiating to mainstream culture, yet still insists on some sense of generational identity. Shapiro also offers some explanation of the context of his generation's drug use—that they were skeptical of antidrug messages in the sixties (their own experiences told them they were false) and that they all grew up with a "benign tolerance" of virtually all forms of drug use.

Referring to attacks on his generation by drug czar William Bennett and George Bush, Shapiro asks, "Am I really a fellow traveler in this epidemic of addiction: Do my affectionate, albeit distant, ties to the 1960s-style permissiveness render me as culpable as Bennett claims?" To some degree, yes, admits Shapiro. He allows that his generation shares responsibility for creating an environment that legitimized, and even glorified, the cocaine culture. The continued expression of this tacit endorsement in movies, television, and popular music transcended barriers of class, race, and geography to reach the impoverished. Shapiro's admission here cites only the glorification of cocaine and also hints at class and generational exceptionalism. The poor and the young are abusing drugs perhaps because the middle-class sixties generation flaunted its unique lifestyle and libertine values a bit too openly. Shapiro, like Tom Mathews in *Newsweek*, does not admit that sixties people themselves have been particularly scarred by their drug use.

The quandary at present for sixties people is what to say to the young, especially their own. The choices, says Shapiro, are not pleasant. They consist of lying about the past, feigning remorse, or "piously ordering their children to read lips rather than re-enact deeds." Shapiro offers another series of possible concessions concerning his culpability for the present drug problem: "Maybe the '60s were a mistake, maybe I too frequently condoned the self-destructive behavior of others, maybe I was obtuse in not seeing a linkage between the marijuana of yesteryear and the crack of today." But even if all of the above might be true, Shapiro and his generation are not willing to accept all the blame. Also accountable, he argues, are politicians who have exploited the issue for years, hysterical antidrug crusaders who have squandered credibility, media that sensationalize drug use as they appear to decry it, and social policy conservatives who pretend there is no link between the economic problems of the underclass and the crack epidemic. As with Mathews, Shapiro does not proclaim innocence for the sixties generation, but he also refuses to plead guilty as charged.

On another generational front, various "old" new leftists wrote of the sixties legacies during this time, often in a conciliatory tone. Morris Dickstein, author of a 1973 book on the intellectual climate of the sixties, *The Gates of Eden*, wrote an article for the *New York Times Magazine* (1988) that took as its subject the same twentieth reunion of Columbia student activists Tucker described in the *National Review*. Though Dickstein cites what he believes to be positive legacies of the 1968 revolt and discusses new campus political issues such as race and expanding the curriculum, he also offers less complimentary observations about the student movement at Columbia. Dickstein begins in a somewhat deflating manner by quoting the former campus SDS-leader's observation that "this is the most self-important college reunion I've ever seen" (32), then characterizes the reunion as "a symbolic reconciliation" with the university "that had recovered strongly from a long period of trauma and austerity" (32).

He remembers liberal faculty from that time who "perhaps naively" tried to mediate between "the stiff-necked administration and the students, who were just as unyielding" (33), and quotes one professor who admits he "sentimentalized the students beyond belief" (33). Dickstein notes that present-day activists at Columbia do not wish to be compared with their sixties predecessors. One says, "We have a lot to learn from the mistakes of the 60's. We're not trying to overthrow the country. Our goals are much more modest. We expect to be living in this country" (68).

In an article in the *Nation* (1988a), Jon Wiener, who also had authored a book on John Lennon (1985), assesses the meaning of the 1960s for the new student movement. Wiener finds that today's student activists do not uncritically accept images and tactics of sixties rebels. An activist at Yale says, "We've learned from the past. The Yale divestment movement today is not just made up of students. Unionized employees and community members are working with students. What we're doing at Yale today is better than what happened here in the sixties" (1988a, 421). This willingness to move outside the student population is, says another activist at Rutgers, an effort "to avoid the pitfalls that befell sixties activists, especially sectarianism" (421). Several activists felt they carried a "media-created burden" of comparing themselves to the sixties" (422). In another *Nation* article (1987, 757), Maria Margaronis noted the same impulse in activists she interviewed who saw sectarianism as the great weakness of the sixties campus movements.

These observations suggest redressive impulses at two levels: First, veteran activists admit to imperfections in their movements; and second, the new campus leftists reject sectarianism and embrace groups other than students, arguing that their political agenda can and should cross lines of class and race that were actually magnified as a result of the sixties campus rebellions.

SELF-CRITIQUES OF THE SIXTIES
GENERATION: IRONY AND DEFIANCE

Certainly the late 1980s was not all darkness for the sixties generation, for no matter how fiercely it was attacked from the outside, it always had known how to laugh at itself. Popular myth has it that the sixties generation grew up with idealism and turned to disillusionment and cynicism in the 1970s when their dreams did not materialize. But the media images and characterizations of the young of the sixties as serious idealists, earnest at best, strident at worst, are only partly true. The underside of that idealism was a deep sense of irony and contradiction that suggested idealism was merely a stay against a deeper awareness that the world really was up for grabs, all meanings provisional.

The sixties generation began mocking itself even as it was being created. By 1968 Los Angeles rocker and satirist Frank Zappa produced a big-selling parody of the Beatles' *Sergeant Pepper* album, which had already attained icon status among the youth culture. Zappa's album, *We're Only In It For The Money*, bemoaned "psychedelic dungeons popping up on every street" as an adenoidal, adolescent voice whined in the background, "Gee, my hair's getting good in the back." By the early 1970s *National Lampoon* magazine criticized the youth culture along with adults and the power structure. The sixties generation faithfully has watched itself make fun of itself on *Saturday Night Live* and through comedic heroes like George Carlin, Robin Williams, and David Letterman. Not surprisingly, in the context of the conservative cultural attack of the late 1980s, the sixties generation could take some solace in the real possibility that the conservatives had not said anything about them that they had not already said about themselves.

In 1987 and 1988, sixties hippie and eighties gadfly libertarian P. J. O'Rourke wrote humorous critiques of the sixties in publications across the political/cultural spectrum, revealing both the broad nature of his message and the ideological dispersion of his generation. A self-described "retired hippie" (1987, "LSD . . ."), O'Rourke wrote for *National Lampoon* magazine in the 1970s and was writing humor and appearing regularly on the television talk-show circuit in the late 1980s. In a breathless style imitative of Tom Wolfe, O'Rourke writes to his generation under titles such as "LSD: Let the Sixties Die" (*Rolling Stone*, 1987b), "Harry, Krishna, and Me" (*New Republic*, 1987a), and "The 60s Kids and the Crash" (*American Spectator*, 1988).

In a section of his *New Republic* essay headed "What I Believed in the Sixties, " O'Rourke remembers, "Everything. You name it and I believed it. I believed love was all you need. I believed drugs could make you a better person. I believed I could hitchhike to California with 35 cents and people would be glad to feed me" (1987a, 16). As for the ubiquitous twenty-years-ago retrospectives on the sixties now floating around, O'Rourke reflects on bad drug trips and police busts and charges, "Sure, everyone says the Sixties were fun. Down at the American Legion hall, everybody says World War II was fun—after a few shooters" (1987b, 114). Regarding his generation's rebellion and ideals, O'Rourke observes, "All of our mystical enlightenments are now printed in Hallmark greeting cards with pictures of unicorns on them. Our intellectual insights led to a school system that hasn't taught anyone how to read in fifteen years" (1988, 17). As for his generation's eternal sense of youth, O'Rourke posits where that has led it:

We're the generation whose heroes were Howdy Doody, Jerry Rubin, Big Bird, and Ivan Boesky. We deserve the stock market crash, and herpes, and the Betty Ford Clinic, besides. We're jerks. We're clowns. We're forty and still wearing jeans. Nobody takes us seriously. (1988, 17)

But O'Rourke is still an insider with the sixties generation, and he reveals that connection appropriately in his *Rolling Stone* essay:

That was another bad thing about the Sixties, all those loopy beliefs— karma, Krishna, Helter Skelter, participatory democracy and all that. I remember when some people were so crazy that they believed the president of the United States was a paranoid maniac who might phone-tap his own cabinet officers, wire the entire White House with voice-acti-

vated recording machines and use a bunch of lunatic Cubans to bur-
glarize the Democratic party's national headquarters. Why, if we had
the Sixties back, freaks and heads would probably be telling us President Reagan made a secret arms deal with Iran and let an unbalanced
jug-ear lieutenant colonel run U.S. foreign policy. (1987b, 116)

O'Rourke takes a similar stance in other essays, too. He refuses to
cross over to the other side. He suggests that however wrong or confused the sixties generation was, it was no more so than those it rebelled against and those who criticize it now. O'Rourke demands the
right to construct his own criticism of the sixties and does not concede that field to the various voices of conservatism.

RETREAT BUT NOT SURRENDER

Essays by Mathews, Morganthau, Shapiro, and O'Rourke respond
to the perceived war on the sixties by accommodating it and shifting
the dialogue into the words and symbols of the generation. They reflect a certain bending to the criticism, in the spirit of reintegration,
but not breaking. In the face of damning censure they do not offer to
repent and convert, and thus they frustrate an easy road to consensus.
In 1980, the sixties generation came together briefly in a passionate
mass-mediated grieving over the death of John Lennon. They had lost
the most prominent living connection with their defining era, and in
the making of meaning they confronted their fractured individual and
collective identities. Lennon, as it turned out, had meant many things.
Lennon as a symbol had brought the generation together in 1980,
so he was used against the generation in 1988. The testament to the
power of a symbol is not only that its followers adore it but that the
opposition fears or respects it. So Lennon became a focal point for
the conservative culture wars of the 1980s. As his death was an impetus for generational memory and reflection in 1980, so he became an
icon for generational and segmental conflict in 1988. Writers speaking to and for the sixties generation seemed willing to compromise.
Lennon was no saint; much of what Goldman said happened probably
did happen. And they could criticize themselves as well as any out-
siders. They admitted to having been foolish, naive, and irresponsible. By their reckoning they probably had more cause for
embarrassment than for remorse. But various spokespersons also held
that neither John Lennon nor they were frauds. They would not sub-
mit to charges of damnation; they would not surrender. Whatever their
errors and shortcomings, the opposition had nothing better to offer.

The sixties generation often has responded in redress as would Lennon himself, by exhibiting a tension between idealism and irony. Aware that the conflicts between the sixties generation and other segments are ongoing, Tom Mathews divines the future in a style typical of the sixties generation:

> In 2060, when the Grand Army of the '60s is down to a half dozen centenarians-and-then-some, the last liberal and the last conservative, the last lieutenant and the last draft-card burner, the last head and the last narc will undoubtedly be out on the porch at the Home trying to gum each other to death over the Last Principle. (1988, 18)

Victor Turner's paradigm implies, though, that by 2060 the terms *liberal, conservative, head,* and *narc* will either be forgotten or will have shifted in their signification so that they no longer exemplify these points of conflict designated by Mathews. We may expect that these terms no longer will provide identity coordinates and that as yet unknown ones will have evolved. And if American society does find a way to "come together," it most probably will not be over John Lennon or the American flag.

SOCIAL DRAMA AS TRANSFORMATION

Near the end of *From Ritual to Theatre*, Victor Turner posits that while social drama often would run its full course in preindustrial societies, in complex modern industrial societies "it is certainly less probable that general consensus on a national or pansocietal scale can be obtained" (1982, 111). What would ensue from social dramas in such societies would likely be "a multitude of models for social order, utopian or otherwise, and a multiplicity of religious, political, and philosophical systems for assigning meaning to the typical events of the epoch." Even though a general consensus may not be reached, the central dynamic of social drama is that:

> Every social drama alters, in however minuscule a fashion, the structure of the relevant social field. For example, oppositions may have become alliances, and vice versa. Formerly integral parts may have segmented; formerly independent parts may have fused. Some parts might no longer have belonged to the field after the drama's termination, and others may have entered it. (111)

Turner also emphasized that social dramas have fundamentally a liminal, or threshold, character. Colin Turnbull (1990) has suggested that Turner's notion of liminality may be enriched by seeing it not only as transitional but as transformational. That is, the passage from structure to liminality and back to structure always results in changed perceptions. So the later phases of social drama, having exhibited various liminal (or liminoid) qualities, would reveal changes. To say that there probably would be no clear resolution to social drama does not mean that the social order and social relations will not have changed. Whatever "reintegration" may be, we may know that it will not be a mere copy of the predrama order. It will involve what James Carey has called a new symbolic order.

American society today is rife with political and cultural contradictions resulting from identity dislocations originating in the sixties. Gitlin observes, for one example, that large corporations claim the right to free speech while antipornography feminists and black activists sometimes oppose it. In words that echo Carey's assertion that social dislocation will be ameliorated in the creation of a new symbolic order, Gitlin says that present-day American political and cultural attitudes are hybrid varieties and self-contradictory: "They have not yet found their language" (1987, 436). The contemporary social drama will not be "won" by any faction, its culmination depends, in Gitlin's words, on "philosophical breakthroughs that are still working themselves out" and "movements waiting to happen . . . movements that do not necessarily spring from the old social categories or speak the old languages" (438).

Analyzing a segment of American society called the sixties generation and its relationship to the conflicted cultural symbol of John Lennon offers ways of observing symbolic struggles over identity and meaning. The framework of social drama provides a way of assigning meaning to such struggles and also suggests the possibility that these trials may generate yet-unknown symbols and categories for a changed, if not less conflicted, social order.

In 1988 the sixties generation came together once more over John Lennon. It let go of Lennon as a symbol of communitas and as a symbol of an ideal reintegration into existing meaning frames, indicating perhaps that the generation's contribution to a changed social order will have been its role in altering definitions of developmental and life-cycle identity forms such as *adulthood, parenthood,* and *old age.* The very attribute that appeared problematic for the generation in 1980—its immersion in youth and problems with transitions to existing definitions of adulthood—may signal that the destiny of the sixties generation is to transform meanings for these categories.

John Lennon was an appropriate symbol. Part working-class rocker, part middle-class rebel, Lennon articulated a resistance to accepting identity forms and definitions from above that characterized the generation that mourned him.

Bibliography

A secret life. 1988. *People*, August 5: 69–80.

After the big chill. 1988. *Nation*, March 25: 399–400.

Alpert, Harry. 1938. Durkheim's functional theory of ritual. *Sociology and Social Research* 23: 103–8.

Anderson, Sidney P. 1980. What will it take? (Letter to the editor.) *Los Angeles Times*, December 10, section I: 18.

Atlas, James. 1988. Chicago's grumpy guru. *New York Times Magazine*, January 3: 13–15, 25–26.

Bangs, Lester. 1980. Thinking the unthinkable about John Lennon. *Los Angeles Times*, December 4, section VI: 3.

Bazelon, David. 1967. *Power in America*. New York: New American Library.

Berger, Joseph. 1988. 60's find a place in 80's classrooms. *New York Times*, May 27, section II: 11.

Blacking, John. 1973. *How musical is man?* Seattle: University of Washington Press.

Bloom, Allan. 1987. *The closing of the american mind*. New York: Simon and Schuster.

Blum, David. 1989. Where were you in '68? *New York*, February 27: 112–24.

Bowen, Ezra. 1987. Are student heads full of emptiness? *Time*, August 17: 56–57.

Boyd, Blanche McCrary. 1982. *The redneck way of knowledge*. New York: Penguin.

Bresler, Fenton. 1989. *Who killed John Lennon?* New York: St. Martin's Press.

Brown, N. R., et al. 1986. Public memories and their personal context. In *Autobiographical memory*, edited by David C. Rubin, 137–58. Cambridge, England: Cambridge University Press.

Brown, Peter, and Steven Gaines. 1983. *The love you make: An insider's story of the Beatles*. New York: New American Library.

Brownmiller, Susan. 1981. John and Yoko. *Rolling Stone*, January 22: 36.

Brueggermann, Walter. 1977. The formfulness of grief. *Interpretation*, 31: 263–75.

Bruning, Fred. 1987. A best-seller's puzzling sizzle. *Maclean's*, August 31: 7.

Bruning, Fred. 1988. The year that the earth moved. *Maclean's*, May 16: 9.

Carey, James W. 1969. The communications revolution and the professional communicator. In *Sociology of mass media communicators*, edited by P. Halmos, 22–38. *Sociological Review*, Monograph 13.

Carey, James W. 1975. A cultural approach to communication. *Communication* 2: 1–22.

Carey, James W. 1985. "Putting the world at peril": A conversation with James W. Carey. *Journalism History* 12: 38–51.

Carey, James W. 1987. The dark continent of American journalism. In *Reading the news*, edited by Karl Manoff and Michael Schudson, 146–96. New York: Pantheon.

Carey, James W. 1989. Commentary: Communication and the progressives. *Critical Studies in Mass Communication* 6: 264–82.

Caughey, John L. 1984. *Imaginary social worlds*. Lincoln: University of Nebraska Press.

Christgau, Robert. 1980. John Lennon, 1940–1980. *Village Voice*, December 10–16: 1–2.

Christgau, Robert. 1981. Symbolic comrades. *Village Voice*: 31–32.

Clarke, Gerald. 1980. Lethal delusion. *Time*, December 22: 29.

Cocks, Jay. 1980. The last day in the life. *Time*, December 22: 18–24.

Cocks, Jay. 1989. Rock rolls on. *Time*, September 4: 58–62.

Coleman, Ray. 1984. *Lennon*. New York: McGraw-Hill.

Collier, Peter, and David Horowitz. 1989. *Destructive generation: Second thoughts about the sixties*. New York: Summit Books.

Curtis, James M. 1987. *Rock eras: Interpretations of music and society, 1954–1984*. Bowling Green, Ohio: Bowling Green State University Press.

Davis, Fred. 1977. Nostalgia, identity and the current nostalgia wave. *Journal of Popular Culture* 11, 414–24.

Davis, Fred. 1979. *Yearning for yesterday: A sociology of nostalgia*. New York: Macmillan.

Death of a Beatle. 1980. *Newsweek*, December 22: 31–36.

Dickstein, Morris. 1977. *Gates of Eden: American culture in the sixties*. New York: Basic Books.

Dickstein, Morris. 1988. Columbia recovered. *New York Times Magazine*, May 15: 32–35.

Draper, Robert. 1990. *Rolling Stone magazine: The uncensored history*. New York: Doubleday.

Eason, David L. 1984. The new journalism and the image-world: Two modes of organizing experience. *Critical Studies in Mass Communication*, 1: 51–65.

Eason, David L. 1988. On journalistic authority: The Janet Cooke scandal. In *Media, myths, and narratives: Television and the press*, edited by James W. Carey, 205–27. Beverly Hills, Ca.: Sage.

Ehrenreich, Barbara. 1989. *Fear of falling: The inner life of the middle class*. New York: Pantheon Books.

Eliade, Mircea 1964. *Shamanism: Archaic techniques of ecstasy.* Princeton: Princeton University Press.

Erikson, Kai T. 1966. *Wayward Puritans: A study in the sociology of deviance.* New York: John Wiley

Esler, Anthony. 1971. *Bombs, beards and barricades.* New York: Stein and Day.

Esler, Anthony. 1984. *The generation gap in society and history.* Monticello, Ill.: Vance Bibliographies.

Evans, M. Stanton. 1981. Lennon and the gun controllers. *Human Events* 41: 7.

Felton, David, and David Dalton. 1987. Charles Manson: Year of the fork, night of the hunter. In *20 years of* Rolling Stone: *What a long, strange trip it's been*, edited by Jann Wenner, 57–72. New York: Friendly Press.

Ferguson, Andrew. 1988. Slimy portrait of an ex-Beatle. *Wall Street Journal*, October 21: A13.

Fiske, John. 1986. Television: Polysemy and popularity. *Critical Studies in Mass Communication* 3: 391–408.

Fiske, John. 1989. *Understanding popular culture.* Boston: Unwin Hyman.

Foss, Karen A. 1983. John Lennon and the advisory function of eulogies. *Central States Speech Journal* 34: 187–94.

Fricke, David. 1987. John Lennon and the Plastic Ono Band. *Rolling Stone*, June 4: 67–68.

Fricke, David. 1987. Yoko Ono. *Rolling Stone*, November 5–December 10: 53–54.

Fricke, David, and Jeffrey Ressner. 1988. Imaginary John Lennon: The true story behind Albert Goldman's character assassination of John Lennon. *Rolling Stone*, October 20: 42–52, 93.

Frith, Simon. 1978. *The sociology of rock.* London: Constable.

Frith, Simon. 1981. *Sound effects: Youth, leisure, and the politics of rock 'n' roll.* New York: Pantheon.

Frith, Simon. 1984. Rock and the politics of memory. In *The 60s without apology,* edited by S. Sayres, A. Stephanson, S. Aronowitz, and F. Jameson, 59–69. Minneapolis: University of Minnesota Press.

Frith, Simon, and Angela McRobbie. 1978–79. Rock and sexuality. *Screen Education* 29: 3–19.

Gans, Herbert J. 1980. *Deciding what's news.* New York: Vintage Books.

Gates, David. 1987. A dunce cap for America. *Newsweek,* April 20: 72–74.

Gates, David. 1988. The "pathography" perplex. *Newsweek,* October 3: 46.

Geertz, Clifford. 1973. *The interpretation of cultures.* New York: Basic Books.

Gewen, Barry. 1988. Stepping on a Beatle. *New Leader,* December 12: 18–19.

Gitlin, Todd. 1980. *The whole world is watching.* Berkeley: University of California Press.

Gitlin, Todd. 1981. The Lennon legacy. *Center Magazine* 14: 2–4.

Gitlin, Todd. 1987. *The sixties: Years of hope, days of rage.* New York: Bantam.

Gitlin, Todd. 1989. Postmodernism: Roots and politics. In *Cultural politics in contemporary America,* edited by Ian Angus and Jahally Sut, 347–60. New York: Routledge.

Goldman, Albert. [1968] 1982. The emergence of rock. In *The sixties,* edited by Gerald Howard, 343–64. New York: Washington Square Press.

Goldman, Albert. 1971. *Freakshow.* New York: Atheneum.

Goldman, Albert. 1981. *Elvis.* New York: Viking Penguin.

Goldman, Albert. 1988. *The lives of John Lennon.* New York: William Morrow.

Goldman, Albert. 1989. *The lives of John Lennon.* New York: Bantam.

Goldman, Albert, 1992. *Ladies and gentlemen: Lenny Bruce!!* New York: Penguin.

Goldman, John L., and Ellen Hume. 1980. Beatle was stalked for days. *Los Angeles Times,* December 12, section I: 1, 16, 18–19.

Goodman, Ellen. 1980. Lennon made a life late, and died early. *Los Angeles Times,* December 12, section II: 11.

Goodman, Ellen. 1987. College has indeed grown costly, but doesn't impoverish the soul. *Los Angeles Times,* September 9, section II: 5.

Gottlieb, Annie. 1987. *Do you believe in magic: Bringing the sixties back home.* New York: Simon and Schuster.

Gouldner, Alvin. 1971. *The coming crisis of Western sociology.* New York: Avon Books.

Gouldner, Alvin. 1979. *The future of intellectuals and the rise of the new class.* New York: Seabury/Continuum.

Gozzi, Raymond, Jr. 1989. "Crazy world" stories leave readers guessing. *Journalism Educator* 44(1): 33–37, 57.

Gray, Paul. 1988. Challenging the myth machine. *Time,* September 12: 77.

Green, John. 1983. *Dakota days.* New York: St. Martin's.

Greenfield, Meg. 1980. Thinking about John Lennon. *Newsweek,* December 29: 68.

Greider, William. 1987. Bloom and doom. *Rolling Stone,* October 8: 39–40.

Grossberg, Lawrence. 1983–84. The politics of youth culture: Some observations on rock and roll in American culture. *Social Text* 8: 104–26.

Grossberg, Lawrence. 1986. Is there rock after punk? *Critical Studies in Mass Communication* 3: 50–74.

Growing pains at 40: As they approach mid-life, baby boomers struggle to have it all. 1986. *Time,* May 19: 22–41.

Growing up with the Beatles. 1980. *New York Times,* December 14, section II: 30.

Hall, Stuart, et al. 1978. *Policing the crisis: Mugging, the state, and law and order.* London: Macmillan.

Hamill, Pete. 1980. The death and life of John Lennon. *New York,* December 22: 38–50.

Hargrove, Barbara. 1980. *Religion for a dislocated generation: Where will those who grew up in the sixties find faith?* Valley Forge, Pa.: Judson Press.

Harrington, Richard. 1988. Meeting the Beatle, again. *Washington Post,* October 7: B1, B11.

Harris, Art. 1980. Memories of Chapman. *Washington Post,* December 12: 1E, 6E.

Harting, Al. 1980. "Turn me loose, mate!" Lennon told Dallas boy. *Dallas Morning News,* December 14: 6C.

Hayden, Tom. 1988. Our finest moment. *New Perspectives Quarterly* Winter: 20–25.

Hendrix, Kathleen. 1980. Beatlemania reached around the world—even to the jungle of Borneo. *Los Angeles Times,* December 12, section II: 11.

Hilburn, Robert. 1980. John Lennon: No secret interior, just integrity. *Los Angeles Times,* December 14: 82.

Hilburn, Robert. 1987. Rock under fire. *Los Angeles Times,* September 6, section III: 64.

Hilburn, Robert. 1988. The flip side of "Lennon" bio. *Los Angeles Times,* September 3, section IV: 1.

Hinson, Hal. 1988. "Imagine": The artist as nowhere man. *Washington Post,* October 7: B1.

Hurst, John. 1980. Lennon suspect still engimatic figure. *Los Angeles Times,* December 15, section I: 10.

In praise of John Lennon: The Liverpool lad as musician, husband, father and man. 1980. *People,* December 22: 26–36.

Januszczak, Waldemar. 1988. Albert and Lennon. *Guardian Weekly,* September 25: 27.

Jennings, Nicholas. 1988. The storm over John Lennon. *Maclean's,* October 17: 40–43.

John Lennon: The battle over his memory. 1988. *Newsweek,* October 17: 64–73.

Johnson, Haynes. 1980. The power of a lobby triumphs over the wishes of the people. *Washington Post,* December 14: A3.

Jones, Jack. 1992. *Let me take you down.* New York: Villard Books.

Jones, Landon Y., Jr. 1980. *Great expectations: America and the baby boom generation.* New York: Coward, McCann, and Geoghegan.

Jones, Landon Y., Jr. 1981. Boom! *Los Angeles Times,* June 25, section II: 7.

Kakutani, Michiko. 1988. A revisionist view of the odd life of Beatle John. *New York Times,* August 31, section III: 21.

Kesey, Ken. 1981. On the passing of John Lennon. *Rolling Stone,* March 5: 22–25, 67–68.

Kornheiser, Tony. 1980. The Beatle we wanted to be. *Washington Post,* December 9: B1.

Kozinn, Allan. 1988a. An embattled Albert Goldman defends his book on John Lennon. *New York Times,* September 12, section III: 15.

Kozinn, Allan. 1988b. Lennon? A film joins the fray. *New York Times,* October 2, section I: 13, 19.

Kroll, Jack. 1980. Strawberry fields forever. *Newsweek,* December 22: 41–44.

Kübler-Ross, Elisabeth. 1969. *On death and dying.* New York: Macmillan.

Lahr, John. 1981. The Beatles considered. *New Republic,* December 2: 22–23.

Lahr, John. 1988. King of the hipoisie. *New York Times Book Review,* September 25: 7.

Langer, Suzanne. 1948. *Philosophy in a new key.* New York: Mentor Books.

Leary, Timothy. [1968] 1987. Turning on the world. In *Smiling through the apocalypse: Esquire's history of the sixties,* edited by Harold Hayes, 328–38. New York: Crown.

The Lennon connection. 1980. *Boston Globe.* December 10: 18.

Lennon has a legacy. 1980. *Nation,* December 20: 657.

Leonard, John. 1980. Lennon energized high art with pop. *New York Times,* December 14, section II: 1.

Levin, Bob. 1988. The magic of a rearview mirror. *Maclean's,* March 21: 42–51.

Lifton, Robert J. 1969. *Boundaries.* New York: Random House.

Lifton, Robert J. 1979. *The broken connection: On death and the continuity of life.* New York: Simon and Schuster.

Light, Paul C. 1988. *Baby boomers.* New York: W. W. Norton.

Lukas, A. [1968] 1987. The life and death of a hippie. In *Smiling through the apocalypse: Esquire's history of the sixties,* edited by Harold Hayes, 339–60. New York: Crown.

Mailer, Norman. 1968. *The armies of the night: The novel as history, history as the novel.* New York: New American Library.

Marcus, George E., and Michael M. J. Fischer. 1986. *Anthropology as cultural critique: An experimental moment in the human sciences.* Chicago: University of Chicago Press.

Marcus, Greil. 1975. *Mystery train.* New York: E. P. Dutton.

Marcus, Greil. 1981. Life and life only. *Rolling Stone*, January 22: 26–27.

Margaronis, Maria. 1987. There's something happening here. *Nation*, December 19: 757.

Margaronis, Maria. 1989. Waiting for the barbarians. *Voice Literary Supplement*, January/February: 12–17.

Marsh, Dave. 1980. The year in review. *Rolling Stone*, December 25: 1–6.

Marsh, Dave. 1981. Ghoulish Beatlemania. *Rolling Stone*, January 22: 28–29.

Martin, Bernice. 1981. Not Marx but Lennon. *Encounter* 56: 49–51.

Maslin, Janet. 1988. "Imagine: John Lennon": Portrait of a generation. *New York Times*, October 7, section III: 7.

Mathews, Tom. 1980. Lennon's alter ego. *Newsweek*, December 22: 34–35.

Mathews, Tom. 1988. The sixties complex. *Newsweek*, September 5: 17–21.

Matusow, Allen J. 1984. *The unraveling of America: A history of liberalism in the 1960s*. New York: Harper and Row.

Mayer, Allan J. 1980. Death of a Beatle. *Newsweek*, December 22: 31–36.

McCarthy, Colman. 1980. But target practice goes on. *Washington Post*, December 13: 23A.

McConnell, Scott. 1987. Resurrecting the New Left. *Commentary*, October: 31–38.

McMillan, Priscilla Johnson. 1982. An assassin's portrait. *New Republic*, July 12: 16–18.

Menand, Louis. 1988. Lives of the saints. *New Republic*, October 31: 30–35.

Merser, Cheryl. 1987. *"Grown-ups": A generation in search of adulthood*. New York: New American Library.

Meyrowitz, Joshua. 1985. *No sense of place: The impact of electronic media on social behavior.* New York: Oxford University Press.

Miller, Adrienne, and Andrew Goldblatt. 1989. *The Hamlet syndrome: Overthinkers who underachieve.* New York: William Morrow.

Mills, Daniel Quinn. 1987. *Not like our parents: How the baby boom generation is changing America.* New York: William Morrow.

Montgomery, Paul L. 1980. Lennon murder suspect preparing for insanity defense. *New York Times*, December 22, section II: 12.

Morganthau, Tom. 1988. Decade shock. *Newsweek*, September 5: 14–16.

Morrow, Lance. 1988. 1968: The year that shaped a generation. *Time*, January 11: 16–27.

Mr. Reagan's way to deter death. 1980. (Editorial.) *New York Times*, December 11, section I: 34.

Mungo, Raymond. [1970] 1982. Three Thomas Circle Northwest. In *The sixties*, edited by Gerald Howard, 472–92. New York: Washington Square Press.

Murray, Gail Griffith. 1980. (Letter to the editor.) *Boston Globe*, December 12: 16.

Musgrove, Frank. 1974. *Ecstasy and holiness: Counterculture and the open society.* London: Methuen.

O'Rourke, P. J. 1987a. Harry, Krishna, and me: Second thoughts on the 1960s. *New Republic.* November 2: 16–18.

O'Rourke, P. J. 1987b. LSD: Let the sixties die. *Rolling Stone*, September 24: 114–16.

O'Rourke, P. J. 1988. The 60's kids and the crash: It's all over now, baby boom. *American Spectator*, February: 16–17.

O'Toole, Lawrence. 1980. The Lennon legacy. *Maclean's*, December 22: 36–39.

Pang, May, and Henry Edwards. 1983. *Loving John: The untold story.* London: Corgi.

Pareles, Jon. 1987. Sounds of discord from Plato's cave. *New York Times*, October 18, section II: 30.

Parkes, Colin Murray. 1972. *Bereavement: Studies in grief in adult life*. New York: International Universities Press.

Pielke, Robert G. 1986. *You say you want a revolution: Rock music in American culture*. Chicago: Nelson-Hall.

Podhoretz, John. 1987. An open letter to Allan Bloom. *National Review*, October 9: 34–41.

Prochnau, Bill. 1980. A strange young man who stopped the music. *Washington Post*, December 10: 18A.

Rabinowitz, Dorothy. 1981. John Lennon's mourners. *Commentary*, February: 58–61.

Reed, Billy. 1980. Beatles injected fun into the serious '60s. *Louisville Courier-Journal*, December 10: E7.

Rense, Rip. 1988. A director's search for John Lennon. *Los Angeles Times*, October 6, section IV: 3.

Ressner, Jeffrey. 1988a. Lennon film in the works. *Rolling Stone*, June 2: 23.

Ressner, Jeffrey. 1988b. The making of "Imagine." *Rolling Stone*, October 6: 37.

Rich, Frank. 1980. Growing up with the Beatles. *New York Times*, December 14, section II: 30.

Richardson, H. L. 1980. For the trigger happy liberals. *Los Angeles Times*, December 12, section IV: 5.

Robb, Christina. 1980. We need him . . . we miss him. *Boston Globe*, December 10: 19.

Rockwell, John. 1980. Leader of a rock group that helped define a generation. *New York Times*, December 9, section II: 7.

Romano, Carlin. 1986. The grisly truth about bare facts. In *Reading the news*, edited by M. Schudson and R. Manoff, 38–78. New York: Pantheon.

Roszak, Theodore. 1969. *The making of a counter culture*. Garden City, N.Y.: Doubleday.

Royko, Mike. 1980. The gun makers are wounded. *Los Angeles Times*, December 12, section II: 11.

Sager, Mike, and Joyce Wadler. 1980. "I just shot John Lennon," he said coolly. *Washington Post*, December 11: 1A, 2A.

Sante, Luc. 1988. Beatlephobia. *New York Review of Books*, December 22: 30–35.

Sayres, S., A. Stephanson, S. Arononowitz, and F. Jameson, editors. 1984. *The 60s without apology*. Minneapolis: University of Minnesota Press.

Schickel, Richard. 1986. *Intimate strangers: The culture of celebrity*. New York: Fromm.

Schmalenbach, Herman. 1961. The sociological category of communion. In *Theories of society* vol. I, edited by Talcott Parsons, 331–47. New York: Free Press of Glencoe.

Schudson, Michael. 1978. *Discovering the news*. New York: Basic Books.

Schwartz, Maryln. 1980. A parent takes a second look: Beatles weren't so bad after all. *Dallas Morning News*, December 11: 1C.

Shames, Laurence. 1980. John Lennon, where are you? *Esquire,* November: 31–38.

Shapiro, Walter. 1989. Feeling low over old highs. *Time*, September 18: 104.

Sheff, David. 1982. Yoko and Sean: Starting over. *People*, December 13: 42–45.

Shields, Nelson T. 1980. New hope for gun controls: Lennon murder may bring young people into the battle. *Los Angeles Times*, December 21, section IV: 5.

Sholin, Dave. 1981. John and Yoko on marriage, children, and their generation. *Ms.*, March: 58–64.

Smith, Harold. 1988. Lennon's "last temptation." *Christianity Today*, November 4: 14–15.

Solt, Andrew, and Sam Egan. 1988. *Imagine: John Lennon*. New York: Macmillan.

Spencer, Scott. 1981. John Lennon. *Rolling Stone*, January 22: 13.

Stashower, Daniel M. 1983. On first looking into Chapman's Holden: Speculations on a murder. *American Scholar* 52: 373–77.

Stein, Harry. 1981. Oh, grow up! *Esquire*, April: 16–18.

Stephenson, John S. 1985. *Death, grief, and mourning: Individual and social realities*. New York: Free Press.

Stevens, Jay. 1988. *Storming heaven: LSD and the American dream*. New York: Harper and Row.

The summer of '69: And how it still plays in '89. 1989. *Newsweek*, July 3: 47–59.

Swan, Christopher. 1980. Fellow voyagers. *Christian Science Monitor*, December 11: 7.

Talese, Gay. 1966. *The kingdom and the power*. New York: World Publishing.

Taylor, R. P. 1985. *The death and resurrection show: From shaman to superstar*. London: Anthony Blond.

Tepper, Julian. 1980. (Letter to the editor.) *Washington Post*, December 10: 20A.

Thomson, Elizabeth, and David Gutman. 1987. *The Lennon companion: Twenty-five years of comment*. New York: Schirmer Books.

Tipton. Steven M. 1982. *Getting saved from the sixties: Moral meaning in conversion and cultural change*. Berkeley: University of California Press.

Tucker, William. 1988. In that dawn. *National Review*, September 30: 32–38.

Turnbull, Colin. 1990. Liminality: A synthesis of subjective and objective experience. In *By means of performance*, edited by

Richard Schechner and Willa Appel, 50–81. New York: Cambridge University Press.

Turner, Victor. 1969. *The ritual process: Structure and anti-structure*. Chicago: Aldine Publishing.

Turner, Victor. 1974. *Dramas, fields, and metaphors: Symbolic action in human society*. Ithaca: Cornell University Press.

Turner, Victor. 1982. *From ritual to theatre: The human seriousness of play*. New York: Performing Arts Journal Publication.

Turner, Victor. 1985. *On the edge of the bush: Anthropology as experience*. Tucson: University of Arizona Press.

Turner, Victor. 1986. Dewey, Dilthey, and drama: An essay in the anthropology of experience. In *The anthropology of experience*, edited by Victor Turner and Edward M. Bruner, 33–44. Urbana: University of Illinois Press.

Udovitch, Mim. 1988. On being a prick: Albert Goldman's last emission. *Village Voice*, September 27: 53–54.

Under Yoko's spell. 1988. *People*, August 22: 70–80.

Unger, Craig. 1981. John Lennon's killer: The nowhere man. *New York*, June 22: 30–32.

van Gennep, Arnold. [1908] 1960. *The rites of passage*. London: Routledge.

von Hoffman, Nicholas. 1968. *We are the people our parents warned us against*. Chicago: Ivan R. Dee.

Vonnegut, Kurt. 1965. *God bless you, Mr. Rosewater*. New York: Holt, Rinehart, and Winston.

Vonnegut, Kurt. 1969. *Slaughterhouse-five*. New York: Delacorte/Seymour Lawrence.

Wachtel, Paul L. 1989. *The poverty of affluence: A psychological portrait of the American way of life*. Philadelphia: New Society Publishers.

Washington Post reporters discuss memories and impressions of Lennon. 1980. *Washington Post*, December 10: D1.

Weinstein, Deena. 1991. *Heavy metal: A cultural sociology*. New York: Macmillan.

Weisman, Avery D. 1972. *On dying and denying*. New York: Behavioral Publications.

Weizman, Savine Gross, and Phyllis Kamm. 1985. *About mourning: Support and guidance for the bereaved*. New York: Human Sciences Press.

Wenner, Jann. 1971. John Lennon. *Rolling Stone*, January 21: 36–43.

Whalen, Jack, and Richard Flacks. 1989. *Beyond the barricades: The sixties generation grows up*. Philadelphia: Temple University Press.

White, Theodore H. 1982. *America in search of itself: The making of the president 1956–1980*. New York: Harper and Row.

Whitmer, Peter O. 1987. *Aquarius revisited: Seven who created the sixties counter culture that changed America*. New York: Macmillan.

Wicker, Tom. 1980. You, me and handguns. *New York Times*, December 12, section I: 35.

Wiebe, Robert H. 1975. *The segmented society: An introduction to the meaning of America*. New York: Oxford University Press.

Wiegand, Rolf. 1980. Reflections on John Lennon. *Cincinnati Enquirer*, December 14: B4.

Wiener, Jon. 1985. *Come together: John Lennon in his time*. London: Faber.

Wiener, Jon. 1988a. Looking back, moving ahead. *Nation*, March 26: 421–22.

Wiener, Jon. 1988b. Crushing a dead Beatle. *Los Angeles Times*, September 4, section II: 9.

Willis, Ellen. 1989. Sexual politics. In *Cultural politics in contemporary America*, edited by Ian Angus and Sut Jhally, 167–81. New York: Routledge.

Wilmington, Michael. 1988. "Imagine" John Lennon on a pedastal. *Los Angeles Times*, October 6, section VI: 1, 7.

Wolfe, Arnold J. 1988. *"I read the news today, oh boy": Irony, ambiguity, and meaning in CBS television network news coverage of the death of John Lennon.* Doctoral dissertation, Northwestern University, Evanston, Ill.

Woolley, Bryan. 1980. John Lennon and the death of the '60s. *Dallas Times Herald*, December 10: 9.

Young, Pamela. 1988. Beatlemania lives. *Maclean's*, October 17: 44–45.

Zito, Tom. 1980. The peaceful man behind the glasses. *Washington Post*, December 9: B1.

Index

About the Author

Fred Fogo is associate professor of communication at Westminster College of Salt Lake City. He has a B.A. from Wabash College, an M.A. from the University of Nevada, and a Ph.D. from the University of Utah.